Nurturing Your Child's
Natural Literacy

Nurturing Your Child's Natural Literacy

H. Thompson Fillmer
Professor of Reading
The University of Florida
Gainesville, Florida

Bill Cole Cliett
Director, Secondary Curriculum
Alachua County, Florida,
Public Schools

MAUPIN HOUSE
Gainesville, Florida

Copyright © 1992 by H. Thompson Fillmer and Bill Cole Cliett

Maupin House books are available at special discounts for promotions, fundraising, or educational use. For details, contact Maupin House Publishing at 1-800-524-0634.

FIRST EDITION

Printed in the United States of America

Text and cover design:
Editorial Design / Joy Dickinson

Library in Congress Cataloging-in-Publication Data
Fillmer, H. Thomson, 1932–
    Nurturing your child's natural literacy /
by H. Thompson Fillmer and Bill Cole Cliett.
        p.   cm.
    Includes bibliographical references.
    ISBN 0-929895-07-X : $9.95
    1. Reading (Early childhood)—United States.   2. Reading—United States—Parent participation.   3. Early childhood education—United States—Parent participation.
I. Cliett, Bill Cole, 1944– .   II. Title.
LB1139.5.R43F55   1992
649'.58—dc20   91-31786
                                                                          CIP

For our families,
especially
our Dorothys

Contents

Preface

*A*n important question any parent asks is, "When should I begin to teach my child to read?" While conventional wisdom might proclaim that reading instruction should begin when a child is about four or five, the real answer is radically different.

The title of this book is based on the reality that humans are born with the inherent ability to become literate. We all learn a language regardless of where we live or what experiences we have. However, since the greatest literacy development happens before the age of five, early language experiences have a profound effect on the quality of our language development. The richer the earlier language experiences of children, the more effectively they use language throughout their lives.

So when should you begin to teach your child to read? The truth is that a parent actually begins almost from the moment a child is born. From the time of their first breath

children literally are beginning to learn to read. They learn
to hear sounds and words from listening to their parents.
They learn to form words through cooing and babbling.

Parents teach their children to read through living. And
the simple activities that most parents—and indeed, siblings, as well—do every day can be enhanced or
performed consciously and routinely to nurture a child's
natural tendency toward literacy. Research shows that
children who are encouraged to do these activities that
develop their natural literacy do become better readers
and writers. This book describes in detail easy ways that
you can nurture your child's natural literacy, whether you
are beginning when your child is an infant, or with an
older child near kindergarten age. It is never too late to
help children develop literacy skills, and it is never too late
to start. We grow in our ability to use language throughout
our entire lifetimes.

You are your child's best teacher

The foundations of a good education are laid in the home.
The success of your child's future rests firmly on the learning experiences you provide long before formal schooling
begins.

Children are born with a predisposition toward language. They learn to speak through constant immersion in
a world of speech, beginning with words that give
meaning to their limited world. They practice these words
through constant repetition and encouragement, gradually adding new ones as their world widens.

The skills of reading and writing should be acquired in the same easy, unstressful way. You can immerse your child in the world of the printed word through reading stories every day, buying good children's books, furnishing writing materials, and providing a role model by reading yourself.

Evolution of the book

This book draws on three recent developments in the field of reading and writing for young children. We integrate these ideas in a program that you as a parent can easily use to nurture the natural literacy of your child.

Inner words. The first of these developments was discovered by Sylvia Ashton-Warner through her work as a teacher in a remote Maori village of New Zealand. The government had chosen books of the "come, look, see" variety similar to American basal readers.

Because her students did not relate to these readers, Ms. Ashton-Warner decided to start not with books but with the children themselves. The first words her students read and wrote were drawn from the their lives. She worked with words mined from the rich native imagery inside each child rather than impose words of little meaning from the outside world. She called them the "key vocabulary" because of their great importance to the child. She discovered that they unlock the door to literacy.

These words of intense personal meaning capture a child's native imagery. A child instantly recognizes them. They provide the proper foundation for reading and writing. When literacy is built on this firm, sure foundation that emerges from the heart of the child, more than mere skills are developed. A lifelong love of reading and writing is established and trust is instilled in the child's innate abilities. The child experiences the thrill of success and the confidence of being in control. Best of all, the child can proudly say, "I did it myself."

Through this process, learning occurs naturally without formal teaching. Ms. Ashton-Warner wrote, "Release the native imagery of our child, and use it for working material."

Whole language. Ashton-Warner's approach to teaching reading was the forerunner of the whole language concept, the second development that contributed to the writing of this book. Whole language theorists believe that language learning occurs in meaningful situations. Listening, speaking, reading, and writing should be taught in natural communication situations, not through isolated drill on individual skills.

For instance, writing is not a product, but a process requiring selecting a topic of one's own choice. A child rehearses what is to be written about it, composing a first draft, revising, editing, and sharing. Reading and writing complement each other and should be taught together. Teachers using a whole language approach generally teach language arts as a unit rather than having separate periods for spelling, reading, writing, speaking, and other language skills.

Cooperative research. During the past several years, experts in many fields have joined forces in researching the physical, emotional, and intellectual development of children during the periods of infancy and early childhood. Working together, educators, linguists, neurologists, physiologists, psychologists, and sociologists have contributed a wealth of new insights.

The results of this cooperative research support the activities in this book because they accumulate evidence refuting many long-held popular beliefs that children are not ready to read until they reach school age. In fact, the evidence suggests that parents should actively begin to nurture the natural literacy of children from the day of their birth.

This book gives you a complete program for developing and enriching the natural literacy skills of your child. It helps you become aware of the many things you already do unconsciously to nurture your child's natural literacy. And it details specific learning activities that you can easily make a part of your home life. These early but vital skills will give your child a lifelong advantage in reading and writing.

Acknowledgements

Books are never the work of authors alone. Many others share in the process, and ours is no exception. Sylvia Ashton-Warner, a great educator and personal friend, provided the creative spark for this book. Her work has long been an inspiration.

We owe a large debt of gratitude to our editor, Julia Graddy, for her constant support, encouragement, and belief in this book. Jack and Selma Wassermann provided invaluable assistance through their thoughtful suggestions. We thank Roseann Russo, children's librarian at the Santa Fe Regional Library in Gainesville, for her valuable assistance in compiling the list of favorite read-aloud books for young children that are included at the end of this book.

We greatly appreciate the information shared by the many parents who used these activities with their young children. Thanks are due also to Judy Voorheis for her wonderful word processing skills. Finally, without the loving support of our families, this book would not have been possible.

*Release the native imagery of our child
and use it for working material.*

SYLVIA ASHTON-WARNER (1963)

*The simple act of reading to children
serves a multiplicity of vital purposes.
It puts children in the
company of people who read,
shows them what can be done with reading,
sparks their interest in the consequences of reading,
informs them about the nature of stories,
and—most important—puts them
in the company of authors.*

FRANK SMITH (1992)

1

You Are Your Child's Best Teacher

*T*he fact that you are reading this book indicates that you are interested in teaching your child to read and write. However, you may be concerned about assuming this role if you aren't trained as a teacher.

Don't be. Teaching your child to read doesn't mean that you will have to present planned, structured lessons. The best teachers of early reading capitalize on the natural curiosity that all young children possess which allows them to learn on their own. You probably already teach your child naturally through informal activities every day. These are the types of activities that let reading develop "from the inside out." By taking just a few minutes each day to talk about your trip to the grocery store, a friend's new dog, the bird's nest in the back yard, reading stories, teaching songs, or discussing other matters of interest to children, you nurture your child's natural tendency toward literacy.

Nurturing Your Child's Natural Literacy will help you identify home activities that capitalize on your child's interests. These activities can be used to develop literacy skills. The rationale behind this approach is simple yet powerful. Children become literate by reacting to their environment with all their senses—sight, hearing, touch, taste, and smell.

Literacy skills develop automatically and intuitively within the mind of each child. What children are able to learn depends on what they have already learned. The richer the environment, the greater the development of literacy.

The words your child uses to describe life experiences are the words that convey intense, personal meaning to him or her. We refer to these as "inner words" because they are vital to the life of the child. Inner words provide a solid and proper foundation for literacy, and you will learn how to develop your child's reading skills by using these first, highly personal, and important words.

Create a stimulating home environment

Rather than forcing literacy through artificial activities, such as phonics drills or spelling lists, it is far better to enrich the environment with so much language stimulation that your child develops an early and extensive vocabulary of inner words. This large repertoire of inner words becomes the foundation for all the skills appropriate for your child's development at each specific stage of literacy development.

Research clearly shows that the greatest amount of learning takes place when the brain is growing most rapidly. And the brain grows fastest at birth, slowing down as we age. This underscores the importance of the role that you, as a parent, play in establishing a rich environment for your child. Early immersion into a rich language environment will help children experience the greatest development in literacy that will occur during their lifetimes.

When considering the development of your child's literacy skills, it is indeed true that "knowledge is power." Research clearly supports the value of natural learning strategies to nurture your child's literacy development to the fullest of his or her potential. Unfortunately, the opposite is also true. Many parents tragically restrict their child's natural literacy development simply because they are not aware of simple developmental principles or don't understand their vital importance.

You, like most conscientious parents, are committed to giving your child the best preparation for life. If you participate with your child in the literacy activities suggested in this book, you accomplish several goals at once. You will be spending quality time with your child and fostering your child's maximum development of literacy skills, while greatly enhancing his or her future success as a lifetime learner who learns for the joy of learning.

Begin to teach your child now

You do not need to wait until your child approaches
school age to begin your teaching activities. In a classic
research investigation, the noted educational researcher
Dr. Benjamin S. Bloom concluded that children will have
already used up 50 percent of their total educational
capacity by the time they are four years old and 80 percent
of it by the time they are eight.

This means that the vast majority of children's abilities
in many areas, including language abilities, are developed
before formal schooling even begins! The implication of
this research is that parents who want their children to
be academically successful must take charge of their education long before they reach school age—and the sooner
the better.

Your child can learn to read at home

Research on teaching children to read is most reassuring
to parents interested in teaching their children at home.
Many research findings and case studies report on children who have learned to read as early as age three. These
studies indicate that when children learn to read at home,
they have someone who nurtures their natural literacy.

Pupils who already knew how to read when they
entered first grade were not necessarily those who are
commonly referred to as "privileged children." These
early readers were made up of all races and socioeco-
nomic backgrounds.

Nor is a high I. Q. necessary to read early. The intelligence of children who begin reading from age three to five covers a large span, from slightly below the average I.Q. of 100 to as high as 160. In every case, it was the parents—not the I.Q., race, or social class of the children—who made the critical difference.

The early readers had parents who took the time to answer their questions and guide their language development. Many of the early readers also had older brothers and sisters who were willing and able to help foster their early communication skills.

Researchers describe the early readers as curious, conscientious, serious-minded, persistent, and self-reliant. Because of their interest in writing at an early age, young readers have also been characterized as "paper and pencil" kids.

The implication of this research is that preschool children can and do learn to read. However, they must have someone willing and able to provide enriching experiences in a positive and accepting home environment.

Your child can profit from reading instruction at any age

To ask "When is my child ready for reading instruction?" is not really relevant when you understand that the journey toward literacy begins at birth. The appropriate question a parent should pose is, "What kind of reading activities is my child ready to enjoy now?" A mother reading to an infant on her lap combines a pleasant and beneficial reading lesson for the infant and quality time for both.

Obviously, infants are not yet ready to begin identifying letters of the alphabet or inner words. But, in general, research shows that children who have been read to since infancy are able to perform more complicated reading tasks significantly earlier than children who have not been read to.

Even if your child is not able to talk well, there are many valuable language activities you can easily do that enhance literacy development. Young children enjoy conversations with adults, being read to, having questions answered, learning the names of objects, and having an attentive listener. All are critical, early literacy experiences.

What about preschool?

Parents who want their children to develop language competence must begin nurturing their child's natural literacy early, by providing a stimulating language environment for them, either personally, outside the home, or with a combination of both.

Beginning in the '60s and extending through the early '80s, much research was conducted in preschools and day care centers for disadvantaged children. One of the findings was that the I. Q. scores of children in these programs experienced significantly greater growth than those of comparable children not in preschool programs.

After evaluating the impact of preschool programs on pupils, researchers Schweinhart and Weikart in 1985 concluded that good preschool programs have both short and long term effects on intellectual performance during

childhood, improved academic achievement, lower delin-
quency rates, higher rates of graduation from high school,
and higher rates of employment at age 19.

This doesn't mean that your child's literacy education is
best fostered in a formal preschool setting. But it does
imply that children are not born with a fixed intelligence.
It also implies that you can increase your child's intelligence and school performance by creating a stimulating
environment beginning at the time of the child's birth or
as soon thereafter as possible—at home or in preschool.

Nurturing Your Child's Natural Literacy will teach
you how to provide such an environment and how to
evaluate preschools for their potential to continue nurturing your child's natural literacy from toddler through
kindergartner.

2

Literacy and the Home Environment

*T*he learning environment in your home is one of the most significant factors in the literacy development of your child. In fact, your child's experiences and activities at home serve as a basis for literacy development.

That's because a child learns words through meaningful experiences associated with those first words. For instance, your child learns the word "milk" after having many meaningful experiences related to drinking milk. Eventually when Mother says "milk," the child thinks, "Aha. That is the name of that stuff I have been drinking for so long."

Experiences precede words. Words do not precede experiences. We stress this point because experiences—not words—provide the foundation for the natural development of your child's literacy. The significant words inside your child's mind, inner words, emerge from meaningful experiences that happen early in life.

These inner words are more than words. They are powerful symbols representing your child's most important experiences. They are words that can play a significant role in the development of your child's emergent literacy.

Parents as role models

You are the first and best role model for your child. When you read often, your child learns that reading is important to the family. Your child will want to read, too. Frequently, when a parent is reading the morning or evening newspaper, a child who is too young to read will sit in the room and look at one of his or her books. The child imitates the parent.

It does no good for parents who do not read regularly to tell a child how important reading is. Your child does what you do, not what you say. By filling your house with books, magazines, and newspapers, you are sending a loud, clear message to your child that reading is important. Such a message is far more important than words unsupported by actions.

Children should have their own books. If you cannot afford to buy books, check them out of a public library. Trips to the library or bookmobile are exciting for children, generate a great interest in reading, and establish lifetime habits. In many communities it is now possible to check out library books by mail.

Read with your child daily. But do not stop there. Talk about what you have just read. Ask about the story. What is the best part? Why? Ask your child to act out a part of the story. Be sure to express your own interest and enjoyment in reading the story.

Prepare a reading place that your child likes. Some children function better in a plain environment with few distractions. Others prefer favorite furnishings, decorations, stuffed animals,or other possessions. At home you can have the environment your child likes best.

Be sure the room is quiet, well lighted, and comfortable. There should be bookshelves on which to store books, crayons, markers, and paper. Make the area as appealing as possible without making it distracting from the activities at hand.

As part of this reading program, be sure to provide your child with materials that stimulate and exercise, rather than repress, the imagination. Paints and easel, paper, wooden blocks, water, sand, and clay are all excellent materials. They call for the child to create something from them. They do not dictate one single function as does a coloring book or plastic truck. By encouraging imagination and preserving the native imagery, you will foster a climate in which your child can tell or write stories and then read them.

Many experts believe that human language development is closely related to social experiences. You can help your child to become proficient in language by providing opportunities to use language. Converse whenever possible. Each morning discuss the plans for the day. Talk about what everyone in the family will be doing. Discuss your work in terms a child can understand. Talk about what siblings do at school, what grades they are in, who their teachers are, and what they study.

Take your child shopping with you. Talk about what you are buying. Let your child select some items and put them in the basket. Point out pictures of the contents that appear on the labels of canned goods. Help your child to recognize various types of merchandise—types of meat, vegetables, fruits, and dairy products. Teach your child to learn to recognize various denominations of money when you pay the cashier.

When you entertain guests at home, let your child help clean the house, set the table, and help with other preparations that are necessary. Prepare your child for the visit by giving information about the guests so that he or she will know something interesting about each one. Teach your child social graces to foster comfort in social situations.

Keep uppermost in mind that you are enabling your child to take charge of his or her own learning. All learning activities will be based on your child's own experiences and related language. Inner words will come from these experiences and become the basic foundation of reading and writing.

The beginnings of literacy

A child is really learning to read almost all the time. You can clearly see the beginnings of literacy in your child's pretending, drawing, talking about stories, conversing, pronouncing words on billboards, signs, and cereal boxes, and asking you to write particular letters of the alphabet. These activities serve as evidence that the child is consciously trying to make sense of reading and writing long before he or she can actually read and write.

Listen to your child and follow up on the interests expressed. When he or she does or sees something of interest, look for a book or magazine that provides more information on the subject. A visit to the beach can become an occasion to start reading books to your child about tides, seashells, beach animals, or plant life of the dunes. Even something as simple as seeing a peculiar-looking bug in the backyard can initiate a new reading and writing experience. By relating reading and writing to such personal experiences, you are teaching about the value, importance, and enjoyment that can come from the written word.

Early writing activities

You will probably notice your child's early writing activities first, just because they are more visible than early reading activities. It is not uncommon for children to communicate quite forcefully that they are ready to write by scribbling on the wall, table, or floor.

At about 18 months of age, most children are able to hold and manipulate writing tools, such as crayons, pencils, and markers. If you give your child paints, brushes, crayons, magic markers, and drawing paper at this point, he or she will enjoy experimenting with the marks these tools leave on the paper.

Your child will begin with scribbles, move on to recognizable shapes and patterns, and eventually attempt forming letters. Researchers have identified definite and sequential patterns in the evolution from scribbling to writing, but there is a wide range of differences in the rate at which children progress through these patterns.

A significant factor controlling the rate at which early writing progresses is how parents, siblings, and friends react to the child's marks on paper. The more enthusiasm and encouragement the scribblings and drawings receive, the more rapid the development is likely to be. Chapter 6 discusses the stages in the developmental patterns of writing.

Early reading activities

Because there is no visible "product," your child's early reading efforts will be less conspicuous than early writing efforts. Yet, certain activities signal that your child is making an effort to learn to read. Some of these activities are:

- acting out the role of a reader
- including books and pretend reading during play
- acting out plots of stories
- assuming the role of storybook characters
- reciting favorite stories without being able to read them
- showing interest in the letters of the alphabet
- identifying letters in environmental print, such as names of gasoline companies, fast food restaurants, or street signs
- identifying letters in his or her name and in other words
- naming certain letters for you to write
- asking you to name letters pointed to
- singing the alphabet song.

These activities tell you that your child has an interest in learning more about letters. At this time you can add some letter activities to your daily routine at home. One of the best ways to increase your child's letter knowledge is to read alphabet books. Any of the following books would be useful. Your children's librarian can suggest others.

ABC, by Ed Emberley, Little, Brown, 1978

26 Letters and 99 Cents, by Tana Hoban, Greenwillow Books, 1987.

Aster Aardvark's Alphabet Adventures, by Steven Kellogg, Morrow, 1987.

On Market Street, by Arnold Lobel, Greenwillow Books, 1981.

Dr. Seuss's ABC, by Dr. Seuss, Random House, 1963.

Bryan Wildsmith's ABC, by Brian Wildsmith, Franklin Watts, 1963.

Other special activities your child might enjoy in learning letter names are:

■ Learning the alphabet song (Records and tapes of this song are available at most toy or department stores.)

■ Attaching magnetic letters to the refrigerator door or other metal object. Say a letter and see if your child can find it.

■ Select a letter of the week. Display this letter at various places throughout the house. Talk about it at least once a day.

Any of these activities is effective as long as it is fun and game-like. Don't use pressure—even though it may be applied with the best of intentions. Remember that learning activities should be informal, pleasant, and relaxed. Pushing, becoming angry with, or punishing your child during learning sessions can actually hinder literacy development.

An empowering foundation

What you do at home with your preschool child is more important than anything a school will be able to do later on. Research has clearly established the fact that there is a close relationship between a child's home environment and success in school. Parents who expect their child to learn and who actively provide an enriched learning environment will have a child who performs more effectively in school.

There is no doubt that you can set the stage at home to ensure success in school. By establishing the proper attitude toward learning and literacy, you will give your child a firm foundation on which to build in the future. Your child will be a more successful reader, writer, and learner because of the early foundation you provided in the early years within the home.

3

Gauging the Literacy Level of Your Child

*H*aving read this far, you are undoubtedly asking yourself, "Where should I begin in teaching my child?" What is he able to do? Is she ready to begin more structured instruction?"

These questions are easier to answer now than they were a few years ago, because language researchers know more about the relatively new field of emergent literacy. As the name implies,emergent literacy is concerned with understanding how children gain the knowledge and skills that help them learn to read and write.

Researchers agree that children begin to acquire literacy at birth. The various stages of literacy develop in a definite sequence. All children pass through all stages in the sequence; only the rate of development differs. Children of the same age can be in various stages of development, because progress happens at different rates.

Awareness of these stages will help you gauge where your child is on his or her own journey toward literacy. It is important that you become aware of your child's position along that journey and work with him or her on that level. Don't push your child for not being able to do something a sibling could do at that age or for not being where your best friend's child is now.

All children are unique and should be allowed to progress at their own rates. Forcing your child to move either too fast or slow can seriously affect his or her progress.

The progression of a child through the various stages of development is described below. You can discover what is appropriate for your child by matching activities to his or her developmental level. We emphasize the importance of working at the child's actual performance level, not the age level. Language develops in spurts and plateaus. It is relatively rare that a child is always performing exactly at age level. These levels are given merely as a convenient way of marking ranges of progress.

Birth through one year

Your infant first communicates through physical association with you. As you hold and reassure your infant, he or she learns a sense of belonging, security, and love. You control the experiences of your infant through the toys, music, objects, and situations you select. Some of the skills children develop at this age are:

Listening. Listening is the first skill children develop, and it is through this skill that most early vocabulary and knowledge are acquired. Enrich your child's listening environment by playing music, reading, singing, and pointing out objects. Even before your child is able to say words, he or she learns to understand and respond to words you say. For instance, you can teach a child to point to eyes, ears, tongue, nose, and other body parts. Soon the child learns to "read" your expressions and gauge your mood. Your child will enjoy having you point to pictures in books and magazines and say what they are. Hearing you read simple stories, poems, and nursery rhymes becomes an enjoyable experience.

Speaking. Children normally will not say real words until they are about a year old, but they begin to babble at approximately two months. They will use all the inflections of their native language by about nine months. When they do begin to use words, the meanings will not be precise. Daddy may refer to all men, bow-wow to all animals, and milk to all food.

As pointed out in the previous chapter, experts agree that language is not developed by imitating adult speech, but by accumulating experiences and gradually developing a vocabulary to express thoughts about these experiences. Remember the example of how your child learns about milk by relating milk to the bottle, feelings of satisfaction, and eventually relating the word milk to the entire feeding process.

A child's environment is critical to speaking. A lag in the emergence of speech is more often due to a lack of experiences than to physical or mental disabilities. Some children do not talk because there is simply no family member who talks with or reads to them.

Other children do not talk because they do not need to. All their needs and desires are anticipated and provided for. These children often obtain what they want through pouting, whining, or "baby talk." Work to avoid this situation. Encourage your child to talk and then reward him or her for talking by responding.

Two-year-olds

Listening. By age two the average child will be able to understand what is said and can answer simple questions, such as "What is your dog's name?" The child will answer when you hold up an object and ask, "What is this?" Directions can be understood and followed. "Put away your toys now." "Please lie on your blanket for rest time."

Speaking. By now, most children can carry on a running monologue to accompany their activities. They seldom talk to people except to ask "Why," respond to questions, or comment about a particular event. They ask "Why" about practically everything, because they are at a stage of intense curiosity. "No," is a common response to questions or requests, and represents a developing awareness of independence. They ask "Whassat" continuously so that they can learn the names of things. It is important for you to encourage your child's questions and respond to them on a level that the child can understand.

Reading. Children at this age continue to enjoy alphabet books, Mother Goose rhymes, wordless picture books, stories, and pattern books. They enjoy holding the books themselves and pointing to pictures they recognize. Heavy cardboard or cloth books are recommended so that they can be handled as two-year-olds handle books without suffering from the experience.

Pattern books attempt to teach children words through the use of repetition. They use few words and repeat them frequently in the same pattern, as follows:

> *Mother, Mother, what do you see?*
> *I see my sweet baby looking at me.*
> *Mother, Mother, what do you see?*
> *I see my sweet baby smiling at me.*
> *Mother, Mother, what do you see?*
> *I see my sweet baby pointing at me.*

Wordless picture books tell a story with pictures alone. Readers can use the pictures to tell a story that is appropriate for the individual child. Alphabet books help children to learn the shapes and sounds of the letters.

Here is a selected list of cardboard, pattern, and wordless picture books that have proved to be popular with children over the years.

CARDBOARD

What? by Leo Leoni, Pantheon, 1983.

Messy Baby. Jan Ormerod, Lothrop, Lee and Shepard, 1984.

Grandma and Me. N. Ricklin, Simon & Schuster, 1988.

A Goodnight Hug. H. Roth, Grosset & Dunlap, 1986.

PATTERN BOOKS

The Very Hungry Caterpillar. Eric Carle, Philomel, 1969.

The Three Billy Goats Gruff. Paul Galdone, Seabury, 1973.

Oh, A Hunting We Will Go. John Langstaff, Antheneum, 1974.

Brown Bear, Brown Bear, What Do You See? by Bill Martin, Holt, Rinehart and Winston, 1983.

WORDLESS PICTURE BOOKS

Good Dog Carl. Alexandra Day, Green Tiger Press, 1985.

Where's My Monkey? S. Deiter, Dial, 1987.

Sun's Up. T. Euvremer, Crown, 1987.

New Baby. Emily A. McCully, Harper and Row, 1988.

Other books that have proved popular with preschool children are found in the appendix. The children's librarian in your local library can help you locate books, too.

As you continue to read to and encourage your child to handle books, he or she learns what experts refer to as "book skills"—how to hold the books so that the pictures are right side up, how to turn pages appropriately, how to read pages from top to bottom and books from front to back.

Your child will also learn that reading is an important activity in your family. It is entertaining and useful. The early formation of a positive attitude toward reading is one of the major factors separating good readers from poor readers.

Writing. At about eighteen months children are able to hold crayons or other large marking tools. They enjoy experimenting with marks on paper and can scribble on a sheet and tell what the scribble represents. Often they say that their marks are "writing," but they are not yet able to associate actual messages with the marks they have made on the paper.

You can help your child to see the usefulness of writing. Make lists of daily activities, write notes to family members, and label pictures he or she has drawn. Talk about this writing with your child.

Scribbling evolves in a definite sequence, which is described in detail in Chapter 6. When your child first learns that a writing tool makes marks on paper, he or she experiments to discover the possible variety of marks and how they can be arranged on the paper. The marks do not necessarily represent anything and are referred to as "random scribbling." This is an important step in learning to write. You can encourage your child at this stage by making various types of writing tools and paper available and by proudly displaying the work.

Three-year-olds

Listening and speaking. At this age children are extremely language oriented. They are interested in increasing their vocabularies and will ask parents to name virtually everything they see. More than 90% of their speech is now intelligible.They use pronouns and prepositions, use correct plural forms, and add -ed to words to indicate action in the past. They use sentences of three or more words.

It is not uncommon for many children at this age to begin to stutter, because their minds work faster than their speech mechanisms. If this happens, parents should not comment on the stuttering and especially should not tell the child to stop stuttering. Give them time to finish statements and refrain from identifying them as stutterers. The condition will usually disappear completely by age five.

Three-year-olds are beginning to understand elementary concepts of time, such as yesterday, today, and tomorrow. They can button buttons and eventually will buckle buckles. They know their name, age, and gender. You can spend quality time with your child by bringing up these concepts in conversations. Ask your child to demonstrate button buttoning and belt buckling. Initiate conversations about concepts of time.

Reading. If you have been reading to your child, the interest in books will continue. A typical three-year-old may also be interested in the alphabet, have mastered many of the vowel sounds, and know at least ten consonants. Your child may not only name as many as ten letters of the alphabet, but may also be able to identify environmental print—the K in the K-Mart sign, the S the sign of the Shell Oil Company, and words on cereal boxes.

In addition to enjoying Mother Goose rhymes and picture and pattern books, many three-year-olds are also interested in chants and songs. They can recognize simple melodies. They will enjoy having you tell stories about things that happened to you at work or while you were involved in a special activity. They like stories about the made-up adventures of a child their age. They can understand stories about non-present situations. They now understand guessing games and riddles and are challenged by books which include them.

Writing. During this period, the typical three-year-old continues to progress through the stages of scribbling. They may begin to associate their marks with meaning.

Four-year-olds

Speaking. This is an age of extremes. These children may seem beyond the limits in physical behavior, moving with reckless abandon until exhausted. They may also seem out-of-bounds in personal relationships, dominating, being bossy, boastful, or belligerent. They show off, are cocky, and noisy. They may seem rude and inconsiderate in their verbal exchanges, talking incessantly and questioning instructions. They find bathroom language and other naughty words very funny. They exaggerate, tease, and tattle. They seem to have more words than knowledge.

The typical four-year-old will talk to pets and toys. You may hear your vocabulary and expressions as your child talks, maybe to your chagrin.

Four-year-olds have a vocabulary of approximately 1,500 words. They use more complex sentences, including statements, questions, and negative sentences. At this stage of development they use regular and irregular verbs—"ate," not "eated," for example—and they are good conversationalists. These children also know their first and last names and the name of the town in which they live.

Your child may recite and role-play familiar stories, and will enjoy making up original stories. He or she will enjoy discussing these stories with you.

Reading. By age four, children's reading interests have expanded to different types of literature. They may recognize words in some of their favorite stories. Their comprehension skills are becoming more sophisticated, and they develop skills such as categorizing dogs, cats, squirrels, and rabbits as animals. They can also describe events in the order that they occur in a book and can recognize the beginning, middle, and end of stories.

Four-year-olds enjoy being read to and have a high interest in poetry. They will enjoy taking turns singing verses of songs and acting out songs and stories. Their dramatic play is now closer to reality. It is not uncommon for children at this age to have an imaginary playmate to whom they read. An imaginary character seems to serve a need for some children of this age and should not be discouraged. If your child has an imaginary friend, join in with the pretending. The friend will eventually disappear.

Writing. Four-year-olds have also gained greater control over their motor skills and can draw a primitive person with one to three parts, a square, and may be able to write some letters and numbers. They are imaginative and abstract in their drawings. They now have sureness and control in their finger movements.

Five-year-olds

Speaking. Five-year-olds use adult-like language and have a speaking vocabulary of more than 2,000 words. They still have difficulty with some consonant blends, such as br, str, and fl. They use regular and irregular past tenses of most verbs. Their use of comparisons—more, most, -er and -est—and other more complicated language structures is limited. However, they have made tremendous progress in five years and are sufficiently sophisticated to use language to converse and entertain. They can joke, tease, and discuss issues intelligently.

Reading. Their attention span has now increased to the degree that they can listen to you read several chapters of a book at one sitting. They may well be interested in learning to memorize stories by asking for them to be read over and over again.

Encourage this reading in every way that you can. Often extensive personal reading can make the difference between a good student and a superior student. One of your roles at this point will be to ask your child questions about the stories both to show your interest in reading and to assess your child's comprehension.

Writing. Five-year-olds can distinguish between their left and right hands and can use them independently. They can draw recognizable pictures, color within lines, and copy words. They can draw a triangle and form many letters and numbers. They can also name many letters and numbers and do simple arithmetic. They attempt to be realistic in their drawings. They now use invented spelling in writing messages to you, friends, grandparents, and other people important to them.

Make an effort to suggest ways that your child can communicate in real life situations through writing. Letters, thank you notes, or even postscripts on the bottom of your letters to grandparents, older siblings, or other relatives will please the recipients and help your child accept writing as an important and useful skill. As Francis Bacon said, "Reading makes a full man, discussion makes a ready man, but writing makes an exact man."

Knowing what to do

Remember that the competencies stated here are only indications or guidelines of a general developmental level for that chronological age. Children with enriched literacy backgrounds develop these skills more effectively than children with poor literacy backgrounds, regardless of age.

Fred is a five-year-old only child whose parents have worked outside the home since he was born. Fred spent weekdays the first four years of his life in a non-educationally oriented daycare center. His parents have not provided rich literacy activities at home. In kindergarten, Fred is just beginning to learn numbers and letters. His vocabulary is well below the average of his kindergarten class, and he has not developed problem-solving skills. His actual literacy level is between ages three and four.

Tyler is a two-year-old boy whose parents, his sister Haley, age 8, and brother Zachary, age 6, read books to him, play games, and teach him letters, numbers, colors, and words. Tyler functions at the literacy level of a typical three-year-old.

These examples emphasize the importance of providing an enriched environment, but not to push your child. Allow development to proceed at the pace and at the level that is most comfortable for him or her.

Once you establish the stage of development at which your child functions, you can use an entire array of activities suitable for the characteristics of that stage. Work where your child is, not where you think he or she "ought" to be. Later chapters will help you select appropriate activities and materials in thinking, speaking, reading, and writing to nurture a child at any stage of development to progress naturally in the acquisition of literacy.

4

Working with a Child's Inner Words

*A*ll the language activities done with your child are excellent preparations for the day you begin more formal reading and writing instruction. It is important that this instruction be based on the child's inner life and experiences. The first words read and written should communicate that literacy has real value. To do this, the words must also carry great personal meaning for your child.

When you begin with words from the rich inner life of the child, reading and writing become fun and important. If, on the other hand, instruction begins with words from outside the child's personal experiences, reading and writing are seen as dull, boring activities.

By following the process presented below, you will be able to identify your child's inner words and use them to develop literacy skills. These words are so important in the life of the child that they are instantly recognized. One look and they are remembered forever. They make reading and writing exciting and fun because they express the child's innermost thoughts, his or her loves and fears.

Because inner words are so easily read by the child, there is always a feeling of success as well as pleasure. You will not have to "teach" these words at all. Pressure or force becomes irrelevant.

Begin these sessions when your child is at the right developmental level to understand and want them. They should happen at your child's initiative. If the child is at the proper developmental level, he or she will eagerly look forward to working with you.

Age is only one factor in knowing when to begin. A few children are ready to read at three or four, while others do best waiting until five or six. Much depends on the individual child and the experiences you have provided in the years prior to the inner word activities.

The important point is always to let your child set the pace. The sessions should be relaxed and fun. If they turn into work, it is time to stop. By following the process given below, you can introduce your child to the wonderful world of literacy in a way that encourages a strong, lifelong reading and writing habits.

How to work with inner words

Now that you know a little about nurturing your child's natural literacy and why it's the right way to start teaching your child to read, you are ready to begin. First, you need to assemble the following simple materials.

4" x 12" white cards cut from sheets of stiff poster board

A black magic marker

Construction paper

Then find a comfortable place to sit with your child. It's good to use the same spot each day so the child will recognize that space as "where we go to learn to read." If you are right-handed, seat the child on your left or, if you are left-handed, on your right. You don't want your hand to block the child's vision. It is important that your child see the letters as you write them.

On the first day start with your child's name. Don't use the formal or legal name but the one you call him or her every day. Print the name in large letters. Pronounce the letters as you write them. Ask your child to repeat the name of each letter after you. When the name is written, say it out loud. Then ask, "What is this word?" Have your child read the card back to you.

Take your child's index finger gently and say, "Let's write the word together." Then trace over each letter. Say the letters aloud together as you trace them. This establishes letter recognition and the correct way to form letters. It also gives your child the "feel" of the word.

It's fun to make up creative stories about each letter or invent imaginative histories for them. You don't want to do this for every letter every day, but, if you keep a record of the letters you have talked about, you can work in some bit of information about each one. These stories will help your child remember the letters of the alphabet. Ask the next day, "Do you remember what this letter is called?"

Begin the second day by holding up the word you wrote yesterday. Ask, "What is this word?" If your child is able to read it to you, it is an inner word. Young children are the center of their world, and their name—what they are called and respond to—is always their most important word. If they are ready for this phase of literacy, children will recognize their names.

Now move on to another word of vital importance. A good question to ask is, "What is the name of someone you love?" Children most often begin by naming a parent (Mommy or Daddy) or whoever is most central in their lives. When you have this name, write it on a card following the procedures presented earlier. There will probably be many names in this category—family, friends, and pets.

Another good source of inner words springs from your child's fears. "What do you think is scary?" is always a good question. Many things in this world are frightening to a small child. "Monsters" are often very real and vivid in their minds.

Words that represent intense likes or dislikes are often a fertile source for inner words. You will get a feel for their importance from your conversations with your child. Events and activities within the family will also provide a supply of words. The more you talk with your child and identify words that are remembered, the more sensitive you will become to what has real and special meaning. Continue reviewing the previous days' words each session before you take a new word of emotional significance. When you have the names of the people your child loves, move on to words that represent favorite things—toys, places, or television shows. You can find these words in your conversations about the things the child really likes and attaches intense meaning to. Frequently your child will come to a session knowing the word he or she wants written that day. Talk about it and its meaning to your child as you write it.

Establish your routine

Each session should begin by holding up the word you wrote the day before and asking your child to read it. If the meaning of the word is intense and personal enough, your child will know it instantly. If it is unrecognized, then it is not an inner word and must be discarded. Do not include it when you review all the words at the beginning of the next session.

Never make your child feel a sense of failure if the word is not remembered. The failure is yours for selecting the "wrong" word. A certain number of wrong words is inevitable. Beware of the temptation to teach your child the word. Remember, this is a child-centered approach. Learning will emerge naturally from inside the child. You should never try to force it from the outside. Force, even if well-meant, will only damage the learning process.

Don't pressure your child to have a reading session every day. The choice should always be the child's. You'll generally find that a child is excited and eager to get a new word each day. But it's natural to have days when he or she is busy with something else. Don't express disappointment when this happens.

Encourage your child to do some activity with each new word. For example, your child might like to try writing the word on a small chalkboard or telling a story about it into a tape recorder. Encourage him or her to teach it to a friend or read it to a grandparent. Give some options, but let the final decision be the child's. Not wanting to do anything with the word is okay, too.

Build on your routine

As you compile a collection of inner words, you can use them to teach other literacy skills. For example, you can easily teach phonics at the same time your child is learning to recognize words and letters. Group several inner words that begin with the same letter, or simply say other words that begin with the same letter as an inner word. Make the beginning sound of these words. (It's always good to start with the first letter as that's the first one the child hears.) If "baby" is an inner word, for example, then help your child see the relationship between words beginning with the letter B and stress the beginning sound of these words.

In future sessions ask, "What sound does this word begin with?" Continued practice and reinforcement are good if done without pressure. If your child doesn't remember, quickly tell the answer and then ask the question again. Your child should always feel successful.

Creating your child's first book

Create a book with the first ten inner words by cutting construction paper into 4" x 12" rectangles and writing one word on each page. Use blank pieces for a front and back cover and staple it together. Now your child has a real book to read and will have no difficulty reading it. This is an exciting moment for a child. Not only is there the satisfaction of reading a book, but also the thrill of reading a book that he or she has actually written.

Avoid the temptation to illustrate the books. This is a mistake. Inner words are part of the heart and soul. No pictures could convey them as accurately as the child imagines them, for they involve all the senses, and the pictures are too deeply etched into the child's mind. If you want to decorate the books, cut geometric shapes out of different colors of construction paper and let your child paste them on the pages facing the words.

A new book can be compiled with every new group of ten words. Before you know it, your child will have a small library of books to read alone and to share with others.

Combining words

At some point in the reading process you will find that your child asks you to write more than one word on the card.

He or she may want the title of a favorite book, song, or game. A meaningful phrase that comes from your conversation may be written and remembered. This is an important part of encouraging reading with inner words.

In working with groups of words, the child mentally joins individual words together and realizes the need to write word groups to express ideas and concepts. Children will often create a sentence that includes several of their most meaningful words. This is an excellent opportunity to teach words like "and," "or," and "love" that the child can use to bind their inner words together.

Children want to learn them because they allow the inner words to be used in meaningful ways. The feeling, "I can really read," comes when complete sentences can be read.

A basic vocabulary of 40 inner words is a good point to begin the transition to writing short phrases and sentences. Apply the same procedures you have been using with the individual words. Pull the words from your daily conversations and begin by combining them with the words you've already compiled.

You now should have some skill in identifying what has special meaning for your child. Write each phrase on a card, then trace and name the letters. Talk about spacing between the words. Discuss the sounds that letters and their combinations make. Encourage the child to write the phrase and share it with others. Make little books as you did with the individual words. You might want to use a different color construction paper to separate phrases from the individual words.

As time progresses, you will move on to longer phrases and then to sentences. There is no scientific way to determine when to make these progressions. It is always important to follow the lead of the child. If these activities seem like work, or the child tries to avoid them, you know you are moving too fast.

The importance of inner words

Inner words are drawn from the mind of the child through personal and individual conversations with a parent. Getting words from a child is easy. Getting the right words—true inner words that are always recognized—can be difficult. You need to be a sensitive listener and skilled questioner. As a parent you will know those people, objects, and situations that have been important in your child's life. Use your knowledge to begin discussions and raise questions about these important things to find inner words. You will make mistakes from time to time, but learn from them and continue the process.

Amy's inner words

The following transcript presents a series of inner word sessions between a mother and her four-year-old daughter:

Day 1

MOTHER–Amy, would you like to work with me for a few minutes each day learning to read some of your favorite words?

AMY–Okay. But I'm not in school yet. I thought you had to go to school to learn to read.

MOTHER–You love to look at your books and have me read to you. I think you can learn to read at home and even write some books yourself. We can stop anytime you want to. Let's make it fun.

AMY–I can already read Peter Rabbit all by myself.

MOTHER–I know you can. You've heard me read it to you so
many times you know it word for word. Let's sit at this little
desk in your room for a few minutes every day at this time
to write words. Then we'll make them into books you can
read to yourself and to friends. Let's start today with your
name. You sit here on my left side where you can see the
letters I write on this big card. You say the name of the letters
as I write and say them. The first letter is A.

AMY–A

MOTHER–There we have an M.

AMY–M

MOTHER–And we end with the letter Y

AMY–Y

MOTHER–Good. Now I'll hold your finger and we'll trace over
the letters together as we say them. Then you may want to
write your name with your magnetic letters on the refrigerator door.

MOTHER–That spells Amy. Now, what is this word?

AMY–Amy

Day 2

MOTHER–What is this word? (Holding up card from yesterday)

AMY–Amy

MOTHER–Very good. Let's start today with the name of
someone you really love a lot. Whose name would you like
me to write for you?

AMY–Mommy. I love you, Mommy.

MOTHER–And I love you, too. I'll write and say the letters while you say them after me. Then we'll trace them with your finger as we did yesterday.

MOTHER–Do you see a letter that's used three times in this word?

AMY–Yes. It's M. I have an M in my name too.

MOTHER–That's very smart of you to see that, Amy. What sound does the M make in those words?

AMY–mmmmmmmmm. Just like the sound I make when something tastes good.

MOTHER–That's right. When something's delicious, you always say it's mmmmmmmm good. Would you like to do something special with your word today?

AMY–I'm going to practice writing it on my chalkboard. It's fun making the m's. They're like a bumpy road.

MOTHER–That's a good idea, Amy. Can you read the two words you have now? (Holds up each card)

AMY–Amy and Mommy.

MOTHER–Good! I'm going to write the word "and" for you. Then you can write "Amy and Mommy" or "Mommy and Amy."

Days 3–10

The mother continues to talk with Amy about her great loves which are always a rich source of inner words. She adds Daddy, her brother, Jason, and her cat, Powder Puff. Her mother teaches her the word "loves" so that she can write sentences like, "Amy loves Daddy." and

"Daddy loves Amy." Other words in this category are her best friend Lisa, Granddad, Grandmaw, Barbie, and Oreos.

These first ten words are made into a little book with one word on each page and some sentences like, "Amy loves Grandmaw and Granddad." The cover is made of colored construction paper which Amy decorates and titles, "Amy's Book." She delights in reading it to family members and friends.

Day 11

MOTHER–Let's review all the words you have on cards. (Holds up words and Amy reads them) Amy you were really afraid last night after you went to bed. You asked me to look in your closet and then shut the door real tight. What did you think was in there?

AMY–A monster!

MOTHER–Why did you think there was a monster in your closet?

AMY–Lisa's brother told us that monsters like to live in dark closets. He said if you don't shut the door good they will come out at night and get you.

MOTHER–Did you believe him?

AMY–Well, I didn't at first. I thought he was just trying to scare us. But I heard a noise last night. It was dark and I got scared.

MOTHER–I used to get afraid in the dark when I was little, too. But you know there really aren't monsters that live in closets now, don't you.

AMY–Yes, but can I keep the door shut good just to be sure?

MOTHER–Of course you can. Would you like me to write monster for you today?

AMY–Okay.

They write and trace monster together. Over the next three days they add: dark, closet, and snakes. All these words represent fears for Amy. She knew each one immediately when she saw it the next day. Somehow, talking about the words and writing them helped her deal with her fears and lessened their effect on her.

Day 15

MOTHER–(After reviewing all previous word cards) Did you have fun playing at Lisa's house today?

AMY–Oh, Mommy. We had so much fun. Lisa's Dad built her a treehouse in her backyard. We got it all fixed up. It has a door, too. I like climbing up the ladder. We took food up there and had a party.

MOTHER–It sounds as if you really liked it.

AMY–I wish we had a tree in our yard for a treehouse.

MOTHER–Would you like me to write treehouse for you today?

AMY–Yes.

They write and trace treehouse, but the next day Amy does not recognize it. It was a temporarily exciting word, but did not have enough emotional significance to make it a true inner word.

Days 16-22

Amy and her mother continue to review the inner words on the cards. They shuffle the cards each day so Amy doesn't memorize their order. Through their conversations they add words that are of vital interest. When they write a word that Amy doesn't remember, it is quietly discarded and the process continues. She adds the names of two new friends in her neighborhood, Jamie and Elaine, her doll Kathy, and Mr. Rogers. The second group of ten words are made into a book like the first one. Her mother teaches her to write the word "I" so that she can write sentences like, "I love Jamie and Elaine."

Days 23-27

AMY–I know the word I want today, Mommy. I want you to write "Littlewood." That's where I'm going to school next year. I want to learn to write it.

MOTHER–Are you excited about going to school, Amy?

AMY–Yes, yes, yes. I can't wait to go to school.

MOTHER–Let's write "Littlewood" together. Your kindergarten teacher will be so surprised next year to see you read and write your school name.

On some days Amy comes to the reading sessions with a word already in her mind. Words like birthday party, Christmas, Santa Claus, and Mickey Mouse are also in this category. Most of these are remembered, but a few are not. Conversations about these words may reveal other related inner words.

On other days Amy does not choose to work with her words. This is natural. Her mother does not pressure her to have a reading session. She waits until Amy is ready to continue her work with inner words.

Day 28

MOTHER–Do you have something you want to write about today, Amy?

AMY–Write, "I went ice skating."

MOTHER–It was fun skating today. You did a good job.

AMY–I want to be a skater when I grow up. Just like on TV.

MOTHER–That would be fun, but you have to practice many hours every day.

AMY–I'd like it. Can I take lessons at the skating rink?

MOTHER–We'll look into it. I think you're old enough if you want to. Let's write your sentence.

At some point in the process of taking inner words, the parent will discover most of the words that have enough intense, personal meaning to be instantly recognized and remembered. This is a good time to move on to the next stage mentioned earlier—to the writing of two or three word phrases and short sentences.

Discussions on the use of capital letters, periods, possessives, contractions, and spacing between words can take place at this time. The inner words, phrases, and sentences can be used to create stories that are easily read by the child. These stories are printed into booklets that become the child's reader. They can be read to other children, to parents, to interested pets, or to any other available listener.

As your child becomes more confident in reading and writing, he or she will begin to create original sentences and stories. The words, phrases, and sentences from inner word sessions will form the foundation for writing. Your

child will create invented spellings for unknown words or
will ask you to spell words for him or her. If you provide
booklets for writing, you can write these requested words
in a separate booklet and start a personal dictionary for
your child.

Encourage your child to experiment with language as
much as possible. Remember to allow the child to set the
pace. You should be as supportive as possible without
applying pressure.

Samples of inner words

Although certain themes will be common to every child's
list of inner words, each one will be unique. The following
are the inner words of a five-year-old boy who had just
started kindergarten. They provide an example of the different words one child was able to recognize instantly
because of their special meaning to him. The words
appear in the order that Travis selected them:

Travis' inner words
Travis
 Dad
Mom
Jason (brother)
Granddad
Grandma
Night Train (dog)
Jake (cat)
Freddie (friend)
Ronnie (friend)
Johnny (uncle)

house
vampire
Count Dracula
United States of America
Christmas
Santa Claus
Home Box Office
He Man
Ralph (toy Mouse)
Battle Cat
television
Easter
hamburger
Disney World
Orlando (home)
Epcot
Baby Snookums (nickname)
Mickey Mouse
Goofy
Luke Skywalker
swimming pool
Darth Vader
bicycle
Molly Ray (school)
skating
G.I. Joe
train
beach

The first sentence Travis made with his inner words was: "Jason and Travis watched television and ate hamburgers."

Emily's words

Emily, a six year old, advanced very quickly into complete sentences. She liked to write independently.

Emily
Lisa (a best friend who moved away)
Jamie (friend)
Kelley (friend)
Me
Mommy
ice cream
rainbow
We took a walk.
My belly button hurts.
I'll be glad when that's over.
Kelley came over today.
Daddy
bikini
Nicky (friend)
I have a new friend in school.
Stacy (friend)
I went to Nicky's to play.

Rachael—3 years old (nearly four)

Rachael
Erin (best friend)
Sara (sister)
Danger Mouse (TV show that she seldom watched, but which seemed to impress her)

The next four names are Rachael's relatives; the words were written right before a family vacation to visit them. Rachael's mother was surprised she would ask for them since she had seen them only briefly when she was 18 months old.

Andrew (cousin)
Deborah (cousin)
Aunt Helen
Aunt Helen's Mom

Erica (babysitter)
Matthew (a friend of her brother Michael)
Daniel (Rachael's brother)
Michael (Rachael's brother)
Eric (Michael's best friend)

Rachael's mother says, "I was impressed with the inner words 'Erin, Erica, and Eric.' Rachael always read them correctly even with the cards shuffled carefully."

Cookie (family pet)
flower
bird
airplane (related to vacation)
lobster
boot
island
seagull
Jodi (Mom's best friend)
Brent (Erin's brother)
Katherine (good friend)

Rachael selected these inner words over a three week period. She had good recall on all her words and was very eager to learn. The biggest problem her mother faced was distractions from Rachael's sister and brothers. The eight-year-old brother liked to make word cards of his choice and slip them in her collection.

Erin—3 years old

Erin
Tammy (cousin)
purple and pink
Daddy
Mommy
ice cream
Shane (dog)
Brent (big brother)
yogurt
Rachael (best friend)
monster (thing that scares you)
swimming in the baby pool
Mimi Majel (grandmother)
Poppy Walt (grandfather)
a new watch
Big Aunt Kathryn
My Friend Kathryn
Brian
Uncle Lee
Mimi Faye (grandmother)
Poppy Stan (grandfather)
color (used as verb—what she likes to do)
the new van
Jolene (new doll)
Happy Birthday (for Rachael's birthday)
my new pink bike
Burdines (where Daddy works)
Miss Lu (lady who works at Burdines and gives hugs)
telephone calls
Wiles Wildcat (brother's school mascot; she has a school
   shirt)

Barbie (doll)
garden (used as verb describing work in her mother's
    garden)
Michael ("Rachael's brother who I'm going to marry.")

Erin's first book of sentences:

Shane loves ice cream and monsters.
Erin loves purple and pink.
Erin loves Tammy.
Tammy loves Erin
I love my pink new bike.
Brent loves monsters.
Brent loves Erin.
Erin loves Mommy and Shane and Daddy and Brent
    and Brian.

The value of inner words

The developmental level and prior experiences of your
child when you begin the inner word process will determine the rate at which literary skills are acquired. Avoid
unreasonable expectations. A preschool child will not be
reading on a third grade reading level in a matter of
months. Fluency in reading and writing requires exposure
to proper experiences and appropriate instruction over a
period of years. It is not acquired instantly.

The importance of beginning with inner words lies in
establishing a strong foundation on which to base future
reading and writing instruction. Through these activities
that nurture your child's natural literacy you will ensure
success and achievement and a lifetime love of learning.

The Dos and Don'ts of Working with Inner Words

Things to Do

■ *Do schedule a quiet time and place for the reading lesson where you can work each day without distractions.* Your child will get into the habit and look forward to going to the lesson. Other family members should know to respect that short time each day for working with words.

■ *Do make the time devoted to reading quality time for both you and your child.* This time should be a relaxed, pleasant experience in which you and your child get to know each other better. You are finding out what things are most important in your child's life.

■ *Do keep learning sessions short.* Five to ten minutes a day is all the time you need. You never want your child to become tired of working with words. A short session each day is better than longer sessions done less frequently. Teaching one word a day is usually enough. Be positive and generous with praise. A child should always feel successful and motivated about reading at the end of a session. If a word is forgotten, say, "I gave you the wrong word."

■ *Do let the work come from your child's mind and imagery.* This source is so rich with personal experiences and feelings that external sources are never necessary. Reading should always be based on words that are integral to the child and hold internal value.

■ *Do let your child set the pace.* The speed of the journey toward literacy should be based on the internal time clock of the child, not on some external standard. Your child's instincts serve as the best guide to the length of sessions and how much should be done each day. Trust your child to decide how fast or slow the work should go. In this process, your child knows best.

■ *Do share your excitement and love for reading.* Young children want most to imitate their parents. When they see that you love to read and are excited about words and books, they will want to share in your enthusiasm. Your attitude toward reading is an important factor in the development of your child's reading skills.

■ *Do try to find and identify a new word each session.* With practice you will be able to separate the words with real meaning from those that have temporary appeal to your child.

■ *Do trace the letters in the new word with the child's finger.* This tactile approach will establish the correct patterns for the formation of written letters. Letting your child feel the letters while you say their names will also help to develop letter recognition.

■ *Do talk about the names of the letters and their sounds.* As you write and trace over each letter with your child, say its name aloud. Ask your child to repeat the letter's name after you. This will help establish a relationship between the letters and their sounds.

■ *Do suggest an activity your child can do with each new word.* He or she may like writing it on a chalk board, teaching it to a friend, typing it on a computer, making a song, or spelling it on the refrigerator with magnetic letters. Each activity will further enhance the development of reading and writing skills.

■ *Do review all the inner words each day.* Mix the cards up each time so the order is never the same. Then, one at a time, hold up the cards for your child to identify. Being able to read a growing stack of words each day will give your child a feeling of real success and accomplishment.

Make up a game with the words. For instance, say a letter, such as L. Have your child pick up all the words containing the letter L.

■ *Do discard unrecognized words.* A word not recognized the day after it is written is not an inner word and is best put quietly aside. If your child asks for it later you can always write it again.

■ *Do prepare inner words books for your child to read.* Use about ten words per book with one word to a page. Your child will treasure these special books to read because he or she has written them.

■ *Do use the inner word cards to build phrases, sentences, and stories.* Your child can string the words together after learning a few words like "and" or "love." These new words are easy to master because they provide natural links for the inner words.

Things to Avoid

■ *Don't begin to teach inner words until your child is ready.* Take your cues from the child. One child may be ready at three while another will start best at five. Your child's interest in words and his or her developmental level are your best guide on when to start and how much to do.

■ *Don't be negative or critical.* Nurturing your child's natural literacy, when done appropriately, is always a positive and successful experience.

■ *Don't take more than one word each session.* There is always a temptation to do more. Resist this temptation. Keep the pace slow and steady.

■ *Don't try to teach unrecognized words to your child.* Inner words are already in the child's mind and are learned instantly and automatically. Just quietly discard words that are not remembered and continue to discover new inner words. Trying to force your child to remember words that are not truly important to him or her will make work out of what should be effortless.

■ *Don't force your child to have a reading activity every day.* The reading activity should be the child's choice and not imposed. Breaks in the sessions will not matter because the reading emerges from your child's native imagery and will never be forgotten.

■ *Don't try to illustrate reading booklets.* These words generate such rich mental images involving all the senses that they can never be represented with pictures. The picture is already deeply etched in your child's mind.

■ *Don't try to do too much in one day.* Remember the five to ten minute limit. It is better to do too little and have your child anxious to continue the next day than to wear the child out in one session and cause him or her to be reluctant to continue the activity. Activities with inner words should never become work.

■ *Don't impose your own words on your child.* This reading method is completely child-centered. Your child should never feel pressured to learn words because they are important to you.

■ *Don't force your child to do an activity with each word.* Activities should be fun and should reinforce the sessions in which you identify inner words. Doing more should always be a choice made by the child.

5

Nurturing Oral Language

*V*ocabulary size is the language factor most highly related to our proficiency in language skills. Vocabulary size, however, is much more than the number of words we can speak. In fact, humans have four different vocabularies: listening, speaking, reading, and writing. Knowing about these vocabularies can help you be more aware of your child's developing literacy skills.

Interestingly, while our personal speaking vocabulary is the smallest of the four, it contains the words that are most important to us. A three-year-old's listening vocabulary may contain thousands of words, yet the number of words in the child's speaking vocabulary may number only a few hundred. Among these are the words that convey the most intense personal meaning for the child.

Throughout our lifetimes our listening vocabulary is the largest. We can understand hundreds of words spoken by others that we would never use in our own speaking or writing. We may not even be able to comprehend them in our reading.

Everyone is always able to take in more information than he or she can express. Parents and teachers should remember that the larger children's listening vocabularies become, the larger their speaking, reading, and writing vocabularies grow also. You can help your child's vocabulary development most effectively by helping to increase a listening vocabulary through conversation and by developing his or her thinking skills.

The period of most rapid vocabulary development

Children experience their most rapid vocabulary development from birth to age four. You can accelerate this vocabulary development by conversing with and reading to your child.

Between the ages of 4 and 6, children develop a speaking vocabulary of 2,000-3,000 words and a listening vocabulary of more than 17,000 words. During this time there are many activities you can do to help improve your child's oral composition skills. Some of these activities are presented in Chapter 7.

Most of them can be continued throughout your child's school career by simply increasing the level of difficulty in accordance with his or her development of literacy skills. Because all language skills are so closely interrelated, you will notice that most of the activities listed under one component of language can be used in the development of all other language components.

Learning to listen

Your child's first contact with language is through listening. Listening, in fact, will be the child's main language contact with the world throughout the first year of life. During that period of time, children are not able to speak, read, or write. But they are able to read expressions and are able to enjoy being read to.

The ability to listen effectively does not come automatically as your child grows older. Listening skills must be developed. Undoubtedly, you can recall an instance when you carefully explained what you wanted your child to do and how to do it. After you finished the explanation you were greeted with the words, "I don't know what to do."

What does it mean to "listen"? While there are many different purposes for listening, there are basically four processes involved in effective listening: attending, understanding, processing, and responding. First, your child must pay attention to what is being said and attend to the words being spoken. Next, the child must actually understand the words or concepts.

After hearing the message, attending to it, and understanding the words, your child must then process the information to determine what response the message requires. Finally, responding to the message means having the ability to make use of the information contained there.

Listening isn't a passive experience. Listening must be active to be effective. The highest level of listening, in fact, involves a meeting of the minds between the speaker and the listener. Such a meeting of the minds requires an active response on the part of the listener.

To become proficient in all four of these listening processes, children must learn many skills. They must practice sound discrimination, that is, hearing the actual sounds accurately. They must develop auditory memory, to remember what they hear. They need to be able to follow oral directions. They must develop the skill of using context clues, to be able to see the relationship of words to other words. Finally, effective listening involves the ability to retell the message, a skill which is the most accurate indicator of comprehension.

Teaching listening skills. You can begin to teach listening skills when your child is an infant. Reading is the best way to accomplish this. Even though your infant will not understand the words in the stories and poems you read, he or she will learn to associate books and language with pleasure. Your child's ears will become attuned to the sounds and inflections of our language. Many of the words of English will become implanted to be used consciously at a later time.

The most appropriate listening activities are those related to your child's inner words and interests. Once again, the approach is child-centered. The idea is to use your child's interests to help him or her practice listening activities. If the activities are based on inner words, that is, on topics of vital interest to the child, the activities will be much more enjoyable.

Learning to speak

Listening and reading are receptive skills —skills we use to take in information. Research evidence is clear that young children who are skilled in listening and reading are the ones who excel in speaking and writing in the elementary school grades. It is important to remember that the more information your child takes in through receptive skills, the more information he or she will be able to express later on. But while children are able to acquire information through listening beginning in infancy, they will not be able to express ideas through speaking until a storehouse of words is built up.

Speaking and writing, on the other hand, are expressive skills —skills used to give out information. Speaking is the first expressive skill that children learn. Even before they learn their first words, children use speaking to satisfy their needs, share feelings, influence others, and obtain information. Initially, they combine vocalizations and body language to make their needs known. They point and grunt, roll on the floor, cry, pout, laugh, and generally communicate rather effectively.

Speaking skills follow a definite pattern. Knowing this developmental pattern will help you to understand what to expect from your child. You might want to review Chapter 3 briefly to assess your child's present level of development in oral language.

The relationship between thinking and oral language skills

Early language development from birth to age three is based almost exclusively on oral language. As children listen and begin to speak, they also learn to think. And in fact, researchers know that a close relationship exists between early language development and thinking.

The more highly children's language is developed, the more effectively they will think. It works the other way, too. The more effectively children are able to think, the more highly developed their language development becomes.

Your child must develop the ability to think before the ability to respond to or use oral language can exist. Thinking is a process, composed of several elements. Remember the word "process" as a memory aid to illustrate the elements involved with thinking. Each letter in "process" is the first letter of a common thinking activity:

P — Predicting
R — Remembering
O — Observing
C — Classifying
E — Evaluating
S — Sensing
S — Summarizing

As a parent, you help develop many of these thinking skills instinctively during a normal day with your child. Others you can actively nurture and encourage. By considering each of these activities separately, you become aware of the different types of thinking skills your child needs to develop.

Although the thinking skills are listed separately for your convenience, please understand that they do not really function independently of one another. They are related to each other and to other skills not included in this list. Chapter 7 is devoted entirely to proven activities that help children develop their thinking/language skills. The activities mentioned in this chapter are but a sample of the many that you can do.

Predicting. Adults know what questions they need to ask to receive specific information. That skill is not instinctive, however. It is developed over many years of asking questions and receiving answers. The process used in analyzing known information to determine unknown information is called predicting.

Children learn to be good predictors through practice. Here are some activities you can use with your child to help him or her become a good predictor:

■ In the morning ask, "What do you think we are having for breakfast? What do you think your sister or brother will do after breakfast? What time do you think it is now?"

■ When planning to go shopping ask, "What stores do you think we will go to? Why? What do you think I will buy?" "Why?" When you read to your child, ask questions related to the plot, such as, "What do you think will happen next? How do you think the story will end? How else could the story have ended?" Hesitate to let your child predict. For example, "The cow jumped . . ."

■ In doing tasks at home or in the classroom, ask open-ended questions, such as "What things will we need to paint our pictures? Where shall we hang our pictures when we finish them? What will we do first? What do we need to do next?"

You can incorporate a predicting activity as you read to your child by stopping at an exciting part of the story and asking, "Based on what has already happened, what do you think is going to happen next?" After your child makes a prediction, continue to read and see whether the prediction was correct.

Remembering. People normally forget about 80 percent of all new information that enters their minds after two weeks. Special memory techniques can help us retain much more information. Young children can easily learn some of these techniques.

When one of the writer's daughters was in second grade, she remembered how to spell arithmetic by reciting the sentence, "A rat in the house may eat the ice cream." This is an example of remembering through the use of word clues.

What do you think of when you want to remember the names of the lines of the treble clef music staff? Most of us remember "Every good boy does fine." The words in the cue sentence help you remember the names of the lines E G B D F. The word "HOMES" helps you remember the Great Lakes because each letter in the word represents the beginning letter of a lake. You can create other phrases to help your older child remember key concepts.

Another memory technique is the rhyme. Who hasn't recited "Thirty days hath September . . ." or "In fourteen hundred and ninety-two Columbus sailed the ocean blue"? Imaging and association are powerful remembering techniques that young children are able to use more efficiently than adults. To help children develop the ability to imagine as a memory skill, give them five or six unrelated words, such as tree, milk, fish, rock, paper, and telephone. Ask them to see these objects in ridiculous relationships to each other in their minds.

Your child might visualize a tree with milk bottles growing on it. Fish are swimming in the milk bottles. Big rocks shaped like fish are reading newspapers and talking on telephones. When the child visualizes the tree, all the other objects should appear with it. The bottles will be on the tree with the fish in them. The fish will stimulate images of the rock, newspaper, and telephone.

Children have greater capacities than adults for visualizing. As happens with so many other innate talents, they are lost as the child grows older if they are not used. If you encourage your child to practice visualization, this talent may well become a useful memory aid throughout his or her lifetime.

Observing. Do you know how many windows are in each room of your home? Is the red light at the top or bottom of the traffic signal? Your child might know the answers to these questions. The power of observation is another ability that diminishes as people grow older unless it is used.

Daily practice will help your child not only retain this ability, but also become more proficient at it. Each day you should ask your child many questions that require observations. As you play observing games, he or she will develop a habit of observing more accurately. Through establishing a habit of observing, your child will acquire more facts, impressions, and sensations to use in formulating thoughts and processing ideas. Here are some observing activities that you might find useful:

How many steps are at our front door? Count as you climb them.

How many houses are between our house and the corner? Walk outside and count them.

How many fish are in our tank? Go and see.

Classifying. Classifying is the process of arranging items into appropriate groups or categories. Classifying organizes ideas and/or thoughts into similar groups. Classification skills are the basis for many other thinking skills as well. You can help your child learn some easy classifying skills, such as grouping. Very young children can practice putting all the knives, forks, and spoons into the appropriate sections of the silverware drawer.

Here are some other classifying activities that you might find useful:

▪ dishes in cupboards—put cups, saucers, plates, and glasses together.

▪ clothes in closets or drawers—put socks in sock drawer, underwear in underwear drawer, and shirts in shirt drawer.

▪ food in pantry—group soup cans, cereal boxes, and spices together.

▪ geometric designs—group circles, squares, triangles, and rectangles in separate categories.

▪ colors—group all items of the same color together.

Evaluating. Evaluating is making judgements based on a set of criteria. Is the product or behavior appropriate? How could the error or fault have been avoided? Very young children can learn to make evaluations if they are taught how and given opportunities to practice. Almost any activity you and your child do during the day provides an opportunity for evaluation. After an accident, for example, ask your child, "Did you see me break those plates? How could I have kept from breaking them?" Other questions that stimulate evaluating are:

Did you like the way Mary behaved today? Why?

How do you think Mary should have acted?

Did Mark do a good job of sweeping the kitchen? How can you tell?

Is that dog well trained? How can you tell?

What sport do you do best? Why?

Do people dress up to go visiting? Why?

Sensing. Psychologists agree that less than ten percent of our brain potential is ever utilized. Sensory perception is one of the least developed areas of the intellect. Research has shown that all of us can develop intuitive impressions and sensory perceptions to a far greater degree than we are doing now. Some young children quickly learn that when Mother says, "We'll see," she means "No." They also learn that sometimes when brother cries, he isn't hurt but is trying to get big sister in trouble.

By allowing your child to practice sensory perception and intuitive impressions, you are freeing him or her to take in a wide range of information that is denied to persons who have not grown in these areas. Some sensory activities are as follows:

How can you tell when John is sad?

How do the people in this picture feel? Why?

What did you think about as you listened to that song? Why?

What does that painting make you think about? Why?

How can you tell when Mother is angry?

Summarizing. Summarizing involves the skill of identifying the essence, main idea, or most important information on a subject. Here are the types of statements used to help a child learn to summarize. Notice they are all open-ended. None can be answered with a one-word answer.

Tell me what you did at the party.

Describe how we made play dough this morning.

What would be a good title for this picture?

Draw a picture about the story we just read.

What did we do last Saturday?

As you interact with your child each day—no matter where you are or what you are doing —you can ask a question or pose a situation that will help him or her become more proficient in thinking. Teaching your child to think is merely a matter of remembering to practice the "process" of thinking.

Now that you know some of the processes that will develop and improve thinking, you can practice them with your child. There are many other thinking skills, such as analyzing, applying, comparing, synthesizing, judging, criticizing, imagining, and hypothesizing. You will be amazed to discover how thinking activities improve your child's acquisition and use of oral language.

6

Nurturing Written Language

Listening and reading

Listening and reading are called receptive skills, or skills that bring information into our minds. As you learned in Chapter 5, listening is the first literacy skill children learn. It begins in infancy and continues throughout their lifetimes.

Listening and thinking skills develop together. As children learn to think, they are able to relate words to their thoughts. They can then attach meaning to words spoken by others. This is why it is so important for you to begin reading and talking to your child during infancy.

Listening to stories that you tell helps your child associate specific words to important thoughts that already exist in his or her mind. As children associates word with thoughts, the words form a filing system that organizes their background knowledge. This knowledge enables them to engage in literacy activities.

For example, every time 16-month-old Tyler climbs the home stairs with his mother, she counts them out loud. After only a few times, Tyler can call out numbers as he climbs stairs: one, four, five, and so on. Even though his numbers aren't in order, he is consciously aware of numbers and is aware that they enumerate steps. This is the beginning of number readiness. As thoughts are associated with words in a child's mind, the words expand the child's background knowledge.

Thinking and reading

Infants and toddlers are able to recognize and understand spoken words, but they are not able to speak or read these same words. Knowledge that writing represents sounds is the first concept that children must grasp before reading is possible. This very basic concept is not as obvious as it first appears, despite the fact that children of all ages are virtually bombarded with print in every part of their environment. Words on cereal boxes greet them at breakfast. Words dance along the TV screen as they watch their favorite programs. They pass street signs, stop signs, billboards, and store names as they ride along in the family car.

Parents read stories from books, but very young children think that it is the pictures that tell the story. Until children become consciously aware of letters and realize that the letters represent sounds and words, they cannot understand what it means to read. But before that can happen, they must understand that the words, not the pictures, convey the story's meaning.

Let's say, though, that a child has progressed to that point. She now is pronouncing a word correctly but doesn't know what it means. That child is still not able to "read." Reading not only involves the ability to pronounce a word by sounding out the letters of the word in a process called decoding, but also involves knowing what the word means in the context of that particular sentence or phrase. Readers must be able to comprehend the meaning.

Models for teaching reading

Almost all reading specialists agree that children must learn the following specific skills if they are to read effectively:

Comprehend compositions

Use background information to analyze selections

Recognize interrelationships between and among paragraphs

Apply rules of English

Identify words

Use phonic analysis

Recognize letters

However, the experts disagree on the order in which these skills must be taught. Three models of reading reflect these differences of opinion: the bottom up, the top down, and the interactive model. Knowing about them will help you do a more effective job nurturing your child's natural literacy skills.

The bottom up model. Advocates of this model believe that reading instruction should teach children to read by beginning at the bottom of the skills list just mentioned and moving up. Children should first be taught to recognize letters of the alphabet. They should then learn the sounds represented by the letters. Next, they should combine the letters into words and pronounce the words correctly, and so on to the top of the list.

The top down model. As you might guess, advocates of the top down model believe that reading instruction should begin at the top of the skills list and work down. Children should be exposed only to complete stories. Because the act of reading stories is so enjoyable, children are motivated to read many stories.

Through extensive reading, top down advocates say that children automatically learn many of the skills, such as recognizing letters, using phonic analysis, and identifying words that are consciously taught in the bottom up approach. Sometimes this model is referred to as the whole language approach, because pupils are allowed to learn language by participating in actual language activities, not isolated drill on phonics, rules, and the study of isolated words.

The interactive model. This model is a combination of the other two approaches. It is difficult to explain this model clearly because there is no precise, universally agreed upon approach among its proponents. Advocates agree that beginning reading instruction should include both bottom up and top down characteristics, but whether one should begin at the bottom and pull in some skills from the top level or begin at the top level and pull in skills from the bottom seems to be unresolved. Because even its advocates disagree on the right approach, it's a difficult one to evaluate.

Of course, the first two approaches have their critics. Bottom up critics say that drill and workbook exercises on phonics are dull and boring. Children associate phonics instruction with reading and tell their parents that they do not like to read. Heavy reliance on the bottom up approach frequently produces children who are so intent on sounding out words correctly that the meaning of the sentences escapes them.

On the other hand, too much of the top down approach often develops children who enjoy stories and would like to read, but are unable to pronounce unfamiliar words. Yet any parent realizes that phonic knowledge is important in reading. The skills most highly related to reading are knowledge of letter names and sounds. If they are to become good readers, children must learn these letter names and sounds.

Nurturing your child's natural reading ability

The technique outlined in Chapter 4 combines the strengths of the top down and bottom up approaches to create a workable interactive model that nurtures your child's natural literacy. This plan revolves around inner words.

Parents using this approach enable their children to develop an easily acquired reading vocabulary through conversations that identify words of great meaning in their lives. The children learn to love reading and conversing, and they realize that reading and writing are an important part of their family activities.

All reading skills are built on these inner words

You develop the bottom up skills when you take inner words from your child and write them. You say each letter as you write it. You help your child learn the sound of the letter as you pronounce it and then have the child say it, too.

Unlike typical phonics drills, this type of letter recognition is not a boring, meaningless series of words and sounds separated from the words themselves. Your child looks forward to learning about words that carry intense meaning for him or her.

The phonics takes on a whole language twist, with the inner words functioning as entire story because they represent much more than a single word to the child. An inner word represents a complex of sights, sounds, smells, tastes, events, and emotions central to the child's experience.

When you use this interactive approach, you are, in one sense, teaching reading from both the top and bottom of the list of skills at the same time. Reading emerges from the inside of the child. It is the most effective method you can use. It also ensures that reading instruction will be pleasant and enjoyable, and that your child will love to read throughout his or her lifetime.

Writing and thinking

Writing represents the culmination of all the other components of language. Listening and speaking enable learners to receive and express thoughts and ideas through sounds to which meanings are attached. Reading develops an awareness of the graphic symbols that represent sounds and meanings. Writing requires the writer first to formulate ideas, then translate the ideas to the appropriate graphic symbols, and, finally, to apply these symbols to paper using the proper mechanics and conventions.

With this technique, reading and writing are used together. As children select inner words for their cards, they gradually learn to recognize the letters and the sounds that make up the word and to form and write the letters. Children learn that certain graphic symbols can represent innermost thoughts and feelings. This knowledge is a key to effective self-expression.

The physical act of writing is unrelated to the actual capacity of your child to invent a sentence. Composing sentences in the mind is the first stage of written composition. Reading and writing complement each other. Readers develop their writing ability and style, and writers are usually prolific readers.

Many authorities believe that early training at home, rather than what happens later in a classroom, is the most important factor in determining how well a child will develop reading and writing skills. When parents nurture their child's literacy at home, reading and writing skills develop together in a natural combination.

Spelling

Most authorities agree that the major objective of spelling instruction is to teach pupils to spell correctly the words they use in their writing. Spelling proficiency develops naturally when you nurture your child's natural literacy.

Your child learns to spell inner words first, because those are the words most important to him or her. You have written them for the child to ensure that they are spelled correctly. Preschool children may not be able to spell the words, but can copy them when used in their compositions.

As children progress, they should be encouraged to use their inner words in writing sentences even though they may not always spell them correctly. Specialists in child development have researched what they call invented spelling. They have discovered a close relationship between the amount and quality of a child's writing and the degree of acceptance of that child's writing. In other words, if you as a parent concentrate on positive comments about the writing itself, the child will try to write more. And, like any skill, proficiency in writing comes from practice.

Developmental stages of writing and spelling

Many parents fear that if they accept invented spelling their child will be a bad speller. Nothing could be further from the truth. The stage of invented spelling is actually a transitional stage that is well along the road toward literacy in writing. Placing it in context will help you see why it is important to accept the spelling as is.

At about 18 months, most children are able to hold a pencil. "Random scribbling" is the point at which their visible writing careers begin. When your child first begins to make marks on paper with a writing tool, he or she is basically interested in experimenting to discover the various types of marks that can be made and how they can be arranged on the paper. Because the marks do not represent anything, they are referred to as random scribbling." Encourage your child in this important step by making various types of writing tools and paper available and displaying his or her work.

When your child shows you a scribble and tells you what it is, he or she has entered the second stage called "scribble drawing." Scribbles now represent things and can be described to you. Children may enter this period any time between the ages of three and six. They may draw the same thing three times and say it represents a man, a tree, and a house respectively. They should be listened to and encouraged to tell all about their drawings.

In this same general period of time, children will also begin to "scribble write." They will imitate the letters of the alphabet, extending them across the page in a long line.

When your child reaches this stage, he or she will be able to "read" to you what the "writing" says. Encourage your child to write meaningfully during this period. He or she can make lists of things to do each day, write notes to you, brothers, sisters, friends, or grandparents, or write about interesting experiences. Be sure to ask your child to "read" the writing to you. Such activities create purposes for writing and will motivate your child to continue on through the various stages of writing.

As the characters of their scribble writing become recognizable as letters, children enter the developmental stage of "invented spelling." They try to spell words before they have learned the rules of spelling. There are even normal stages of development within this period, too.

In the first stage, they spell using consonants only, representing whole words with either the first or last consonant of the word. Dick will be either D or K. Soon they will use both the beginning and ending consonants, and Dick will be written DK.

As they begin to spell phonetically, children acknowledge vowel as well as consonant phonemes or sounds. Now Dick may be DIK. Four-year-old Zachary, for example, has a sister, Haley, aged seven. When they were very young, Zac and Haley's mother taught them that writing is a great way to communicate. The children take turns feeding a pet fish. One day, Zac could not remember whose turn it was, so he fed the fish and left Haley this note on her door:

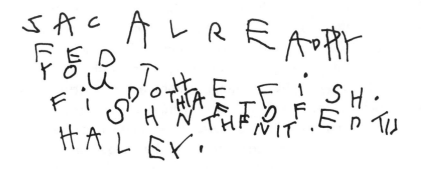

*Zac already fed the fish. You don't have to feed
the fish in the night, Haley.*

The spelling was certainly invented, but the meaning is
clear. After children enter the primary grades, they begin a
stage of "transitional" spelling. They realize that there is
not a one-to-one correspondence between letters and
sounds. They write words, such as BAER for bear, KAEP as
cape, and RALLE for rail.

By third grade most children have learned the standard
rules for spelling in our language and enter the conventional stage of spelling. Except for a few difficult words,
they spell most of the words they use in their writing
correctly.

Accept invented spelling

If you understand that invented spelling is just one stage along the way toward learning how to write, it's easier to accept it. Since children acquire literacy by participating in meaningful language situations, you nurture their natural literacy by encouraging them to write every day, spelling words as they think they should be spelled.

Your child sees and learns correct spelling when you copy inner words, and he or she will begin to notice how they are spelled through your reading together. But in your child's own writing, accept the words as they are written. To insist on correct spellings only frustrates your child's early attempts, and in fact, inhibits his or her desire to express personal thoughts and feelings in writing.

Spelling researchers find that children use more words in their writing when their invented spelling is accepted without comment by adults. Research evidence indicates that by the end of third grade there is no difference in the conventional spelling ability between invented spellers and children who have been encouraged to spell every word correctly. But invented spellers use a wider range of words in their writing, evidently because they have not been discouraged from using words they cannot spell.

Encourage your child to write stories, keep a journal, make lists, write letters to relatives and friends, and do any other kinds of writing that seem to be of interest. Continue to write inner words correctly and spell words for your child upon request. But do not correct the spelling of words your preschooler uses in writing.

Working with mechanics

As older children begin to write sentences, parents can help them learn the correct use of capital letters, punctuation marks, apostrophes to show contractions and possessives, and spacing between words. As your child becomes more proficient in forming letters, you can offer suggestions that will help to improve handwriting. You must remember, however, that the ability to form letters depends upon small motor skill refinement. By all means demonstrate how to form the letters and encourage writing every day, but do not become impatient if your child does not form the letters well. It may be that your child's small motor skills have not developed sufficiently to perform these tasks.

Usage

Continue to help with mechanics when your child begins to write paragraphs. At that point, you can also begin to help develop an awareness of grammar and usage. Practice using adjectives and adverbs to help your child make sentences more descriptive. Provide information also on how to make subjects and verbs agree and to make pronouns agree with the words for which they stand.

All suggestions for improving compositions should be made in a helpful, non-critical manner. It is better to ignore a young child's errors in mechanics temporarily than to cause frustration by insisting on too many corrections. Again, realize that lessons about usage and mechanics will be generally reserved for a child who is at least eight or nine.

Word Processing

If you own a computer with a word processing program, you can encourage your child to use it to practice writing. Children who have trouble forming the letters with a pencil often enjoy typing them on the keyboard.

As children become more skillful with the word processor and in working with their inner words, they can compose sentences and, later, stories. One of the great advantages of composing on a computer is that children can edit as they write without rewriting large segments of the composition as they must do with pencil and paper. Once again, accept non-standard spelling as your child explores new words.

Composing

As children learn to combine words into sentences and to then combine sentences into stories, they are composing. By nurturing reading from the inside of your child out into the world, you will find that a child's writing skills flourish in creative and literary-skillful ways.

Through actual experience, children learn that what they know about, they can think about; what they think about, they can talk about; what they talk about, they can write about; what they write about, they can read about.

This technique of teaching reading by nurturing your child's' natural literacy provides experiences in all these components of language at once. No one language skill is presented in isolation. Children learn that language skills cannot be separated but are all closely related to each other. As they gain proficiency in one skill, this proficiency enables them to improve their competencies in all the other skills. These integrated experiences empower them to value learning and to try to express themselves as precisely as possible.

Revising

When children are able to write their own compositions, they use all the language skills. What they have thought, they have spoken. What they have spoken, they have written. What they have written, they can read. Eventually, they will become advanced enough in writing to criticize their own work. They will learn to edit and revise their writing so that it expresses their thoughts more effectively.

Be supportive of your child's efforts to improve. Encourage self-evaluation of writing. You should help with mechanics and usage only when requested to do so. Allow your child to decide what parts of the writing to revise. Through experience in writing, he or she will become conscious of the following techniques used by good writers:

Choosing a title that makes the reader want to read the composition

Using the first sentence to involve the reader in the story

Telling the story in the appropriate sequence

Selecting words that are exciting and colorful

Using direct quotations where appropriate

Creating desirable effects by using figures of speech

Choosing an effective ending for the composition.

Be supportive of your child's efforts to edit and revise writing to more effectively express thoughts. It is important for him or her to understand that writers usually rewrite what they write and that a first draft is seldom the final version.

7

Activities that Nurture Language

*A*ll children experience the need to engage in certain activities that contribute to their development at that particular stage. When you nurture your child's natural literacy with activities appropriate to his or her developmental level, you essentially free your child to learn to read through normal, child-like activities.

For example, at around 18 months many children experience a need to begin using tools in their hands to make marks. If no marking tools are available, the child will not be able to practice "writing." They may not proceed through the writing stages as rapidly as a child whose parents made writing tools available.

You can easily satisfy your child's need to experiment with writing by providing appropriate materials and showing your child how to use them. Once you have done that, the child will take it from there. Some writing tools you may want to make available are:

A child-size easel

Finger paints and slick paper on which to smear paint

Tablet(s) of newsprint (inexpensive drawing paper)

Crayons, large pencils, washable markers, etch-o-sketch board, and other drawing tools

Watercolors and brushes.

Reading stories

Four-year-old Matthew and his 18-month-old sister, Rebecca, have parents who began reading to them when they were infants. Matthew now has his own collection of books, knows their titles, and can recite entire stories from most of the books from memory. He can also read many words from each story. Rebecca has her own collection of books, and can locate each of them by title. She cannot recite words as Matthew can, but she can point to some of the words upon request. Both children are now "reading" at the peak of their potential for their age.

Although Matthew and Rebecca have had no formal reading instruction, their parents nurtured their natural literacy. They read to them individually and allowed them to participate in the reading as fully as their ability and desire permitted. They applied no pressure to perform. They showed by example that reading is an enjoyable activity, allowing the children to participate as much or as little as they chose. Given such options, most children choose to participate extensively in reading activities because it gives them pleasant, quality time with their parents.

Reading is an activity you can do with your child for a short period of time every day. You may not even view such an activity as teaching, but it is. There are hundreds of similar activities that are fun for you and your child that will help develop skills in thinking, listening, speaking, reading, and writing. Many activities develop skills in all five of these areas at the same time.

General information

Research shows that the most successful children in kindergarten are those with the most extensive storehouse of general information. These are pupils who know where their parents work; the grade level of their brother/ sister; letters, numbers, colors, common animals; and other general information. These children generally have enough background knowledge to learn to read. They begin their school career with a definite advantage. Remember, future learning is based on what the child already knows. A few examples of activities that build background knowledge are:

Learning about the family. Include your child in family planning sessions. Children enjoy participating in discussions about what the family should do next Saturday afternoon; what present to buy for Grandma's birthday; where Mother is taking Mary to buy a new blouse for her piano recital; and who will take the dog for his rabies shot.

Not only does participation in family discussions make your child feel like an important part of the family, but it causes him or her to develop an interest in what other members are doing. Participation in planning also helps your child to learn both the importance of and the strategies used in making plans.

Your child should also be taught important information about your family, like:

- Where do you work and what do you do at work?

- What are some activities in which parents and siblings participate on a regular basis, such as organizations, sports, and volunteering?

- What school does sister or brother attend, in what grade is he/she, and what activities does he or she do there?

- What is your street address and telephone number?

- In what city, county, and state do you live?

Other information your child can learn includes:

Learning about animals

- Visit a pet store, humane society, farm, ranch, or zoo to teach about various types of animals.

- Show pictures of the animals your child has seen.

- Give your child a pet to care for. Read a book about what the pet eats, how often it eats, and how to groom and train the pet.

Learning about colors

■ Point to objects and tell what color they are.

■ Hold a different colored marble in each hand and ask the child to pick the hand holding the red marble.

■ Ask your child to draw objects in particular colors.

■ Describe clothing by color: "Put on your red socks."

■ Create a color by mixing two other colors.

■ Ask your child to find colored objects in pictures—find a blue drum, a yellow sock, or a brown dog.

■ Obtain a color chart from a paint store and ask your child to point to particular colors.

Measuring activities

■ Play with measuring instruments and have your child pour sand from measuring cups to learn the concepts of half, quarter, and third.

■ With a tape measure, have your child measure his or her height and find the length of the leg, arm, thumb, and fingers.

■ With cups, glasses, and pans, help your child find how many cups of water it takes to fill different sized glasses and pans.

■ Build a bird feeder or other wood project. Ask your child to measure the pieces. Have him or her assemble them prior to nailing to show how they fit.

■ Give your child children's jigsaw puzzles and help him or her assemble them.

Listening and speaking skills

Listening is the first literacy skill that your child will use. Newly-born infants of all cultures begin to sort out the particular rhythms, rhymes, and melodies of their language through hearing the language spoken, regardless of the language. Greek children learn Greek. Japanese children learn Japanese. Your child will learn the characteristics of your language much more quickly and effectively, however, if you provide many opportunities to listen to the language by talking and singing to him or her regularly throughout the day.

Reading aloud is an especially effective strategy for literacy development, even for infants. As your child grows older and begins to talk, you can continue to help him or her to develop effective listening and speaking skills by using some of the following activities:

Discriminating between sounds. To listen effectively children must hear sounds correctly. Learning to discriminate between sounds will also improve pronunciation skills. The following games can help your child learn to discriminate between sounds:

■ "Listen carefully as I say a sentence with the last word missing. You pick a word that will make the sentence rhyme."

"I saw a rat who was wearing a _____."

"Go into the hall and play with your _____."

"Raise your hand up high and try to touch the _____."

"Because it was night, we turned on the _____."

"I picked up a broom and swept out my _____."

■ Here's another, called "Listen carefully and tell me what I am doing."

You stand where your child cannot see you and do a number of activities that make different noises. Your child must both hear and describe the sound accurately. These tasks might include wrinkling a sheet of paper, ringing a small bell, blowing a whistle, dropping a coin on the floor, clapping your hands, whistling, or tapping a pencil.

Improving auditory memory. To be effective listeners children must remember what they hear in a process called auditory memory. Here are some activities to help improve auditory memory if your child is three or older:

■ Say a series of four numbers and ask your child to repeat them. Gradually increase the numbers to see how many your child can remember.

To vary this activity, say the numbers and ask your child to say them in reverse order. If you say 7486, your child should say 6847. Children are not able to repeat as many numbers in reverse order as they can in natural order.

■ Tap a rhythm with a pencil and have your child repeat the same rhythm after you. Change the rhythm each time.

■ Read a simple rhyme or limerick. Ask your child to repeat it.

■ Say aloud four or five words and ask your child to repeat the words in the order that you said them.

■ Play the Suitcase Game. "I am going on a trip and I will take a toothbrush in my suitcase." Your child responds, "I am going on a trip and I will take a toothbrush and a comb in my suitcase." Each player must repeat all the items previously mentioned and add one. The game ends when someone forgets an item mentioned before.

■ Play the alphabet game, "I went to the store and bought some apples. The next player adds an item beginning with B...etc. and repeats all words mentioned before in order.

Following oral directions. The ability to follow oral directions represents "responding," which is the highest level of listening. The following activities will help your child to listen and respond appropriately to oral directions:

■ Play "Simon Says" or any other game that requires responding to oral directions.

■ Explain or read the directions to a card game or board game that your child is mature enough to play. Ask your child to explain the directions to ensure understanding before playing the game.

■ Ask your child to give you oral directions on how to use a VCR, walk to a friend's house, or prepare a recipe.

Using context clues. To understand both oral and written information, children must be able to see the relationship of words to other words. The following activities will help your child to use appropriate words in sentences:

■ Read aloud a story, poem, or nursery rhyme that your child knows. Omit an important word every few sentences. Ask your child to furnish the missing word. If your child doesn't respond immediately, furnish the word and continue to read.

■ Make up a sentence containing a word your child does not know. Say the sentence aloud and ask your child to guess what the word means. Ask your child to tell how the other words provided clues to the meaning of the unknown word. A sample sentence might be, "She was so sad that she wept."

Retelling spoken messages. Retelling is one of the most accurate ways to discover whether your child understands a message. Children can improve this skill through practice. Here are some activities to develop your child's understanding of messages:

■ Read aloud a myth, fairy tale, or very short story. Ask your child to retell the story.

■ Watch an episode on a children's TV program with your child and then discuss it.

■ Record a story on tape. Ask your child to listen to the story once and then retell it. Your child should record the retelling of the story on the same tape.

Responding. Your child can practice both listening and speaking by restating or reciting any information presented either orally or in writing. Reciting poems and nursery rhymes, retelling stories or experiences, and reporting on their sensory perceptions as they listened to a story can improve your child's listening and speaking skills. The greater the variety and frequency of these experiences your child has, the more effectively he or she will learn to listen and speak.

Reading and writing skills

Reading and writing are closely related to listening and speaking. Like listening, reading is a receptive skill. Like speaking, writing is an expressive skill. Your child reads to take in information and writes to express information.

All the activities listed under listening and speaking skills help prepare your child to read and write. Some of the skills researchers have found to be closely associated with reading and writing are grouped under their appropriate classifications below.

Decoding skills. These skills enable the child to recognize and interpret letters and letter sounds. They include:

■ Learning the names of the letters.

■ Identifying letter sounds.

■ Pronouncing letter combinations, such as bl, ch, ou, and ea.

■ Using phonemic segmentation, a fancy way of explaining the recognition of the phonetic make-up of a word. For example, recognizing that "cat" is pronounced by combining the three sounds: \c\, \a\, and \t\.

■ Using word attack skills— recognizing prefixes, root words, compound words, and suffixes.

Learning complicated skills unconsciously

The lists above may seem rather complicated, but your child can learn to perform them all unconsciously if language activities are appropriate and interesting. As you nurture your child's natural literacy, keep the following three facts uppermost in your mind:

(1) children learn to read by reading, and children learn to write by writing;

(2) children want to learn to read when they see their parents read, and they want to learn to write when they see their parents write; and

(3) children learn to read and write when their parents provide appropriate experiences and work with them each day to make learning an adventure.

All the skills involved in thinking, speaking, listening, reading, and writing are learned as children reveal their inner words, write them, read them, form them into sentences, and later into stories. Parents who are able to learn their children's inner words find out what things, thoughts, and activities are most important to them. These parents share in the important people and events around which their children's lives revolve. Not only do these parents teach their children to read, but they also establish enduring, positive, and caring relationships with them.

8

Selecting a Preschool that Nutures Literacy

*M*ost communities support preschools with differing organizational structures and philosophies of education. Schools that serve children aged five or under are usually called day care centers, nursery schools, or preschools.

Day care centers generally provide babysitting services and basic child care. On the other hand, nurseries or preschools usually add some type of educational environment. Both types of schools can be found in private homes, churches or temples, in business or industrial workplaces, and on college or university campuses.

Need for preschool

As a nation, America needs good preschools. About 20 million children in the U.S. today are under the age of 5. Nearly 60 percent of the mothers of these children work outside the home. Almost one out of every five of these children come from a single parent home headed by a female. While many of the children in preschool facilities are there through necessity, a large number are enrolled through parental choice.

To preschool or not?

If you are not employed outside the home or have no other pressing need that requires you to send your child away from home during the day, should you consider doing so? Parents who do say that chose preschool for a variety of positive reasons.

They believe that a preschool will help their child learn to function in a structured situation; become more independent and self assured; improve physical and intellectual development; meet and learn to interact with other children; improve communication skills; and experience an enriched and stimulating environment with time away from parents and siblings.

Other parents in the same situation believe that preschool isn't right for their child. They prefer having their child at home, or their child may not want to go to preschool. They may not be able to afford preschool or to find one they like. These parents believe they can provide their child with the same types of experiences available in the local preschools and prefer to decide what kinds of experiences their child will have.

A decision to send a child to preschool is a personal one. Neither precludes your child from getting the best start he or she needs in literacy development.

Locating a preschool

If you decide preschool is right for your child, finding one in your community usually isn't difficult. Recommendations from friends are probably the best way to find a preschool you like, but you can always resort to the telephone directory or newspaper ads, too.

The hard part comes after you have collected information on the types of preschools available in your community: evaluating them to decide which one is right for your child and you. Even if there are dozens of preschools in your community, there may be few that offer the type of program you want. Their differences will help you to begin narrowing your choices based on your own needs.

For example, some preschools meet half a day while others meet a full day. Some cater to a restricted age group only while others enroll pupils with a wide age range. Some preschools do little more than babysit while others offer impressive educational programs. Some employ professional educators while others have managers who may be assisted by untrained workers.

Evaluating a preschool

Decide first whether you want an educational experience or a primarily social, babysitting situation. That done, you can begin to evaluate specific facilities. Remember that cost is not always a sign of quality in preschools. Educational preschools are usually more expensive than child care facilities, but this isn't always true. It is quite possible, for instance, that an excellent church or public school-sponsored educational program will charge the same or less than a child care center. Here are some factors to consider when selecting a preschool for your child.

Licensing requirements. If you live in a state or community that requires preschools to be licensed, do not consider a school that is not licensed to operate! These schools do exist, but they are not legal and may not meet state requirements. Bear in mind, also, that just because a preschool is licensed, that alone is no guarantee it is a good school. It only means that it meets the requirements for licensing.

Not all states, however, require preschools to be licensed. If you live in such a state, the guidelines in this chapter will be even more helpful in your quest to find the program that is best for your child and you.

Educational philosophy. This is the single most important aspect of a potential preschool for your child. If you are not in agreement with that aspect of the school, drop it from consideration. In Chapter 6 you learned that there are three models for teaching reading: the bottom up, the top down, and the interactive. These same models can be used to describe the general educational philosophies of preschools. In bottom-up preschools you will see all the children working on the same thing at the same time. They may all be given a picture to color. The teacher and aides circulate around the room and help children perform their tasks correctly. When the children have finished coloring the picture, they may be given a worksheet showing incomplete letters of the alphabet. Then, they will "close up" the spaces with a pencil or crayon to make a complete letter. They may all perform the same exercises in physical education class or recess. After recess, they may sit in a group and sing. Basically, the entire school day is organized in this fashion.

This preschool type, like the bottom up reading model, places the emphasis on learning basic skills: drawing, letter-naming, jumping, and learning words to songs. Although children have opportunities for play during the day, more time is devoted to formal instruction.

The philosophy is skill or content oriented, centered on and organized around the content to be learned rather than around the children. Children begin with the basic skills or content because this philosophy holds that this is necessary for children to work up to higher level skills.

On the other hand, in a top down preschool you will see children at work on different projects. There will be no worksheets. Instead, you will notice many interest areas, such as a dress-up corner, a reading area, painting area, kitchen, and toy area throughout the room. There are few organized activities, a flexible schedule, and little formal instruction.

This type of classroom is organized around the interests of children. It is child-centered. Children choose the activities they are interested in. Teachers and aides help or participate with children in whatever activity they are doing.

Most of the activities revolve around play, unlike those in the bottom up preschool. As children perform activities that are meaningful to them, they develop the basic skills involved in performing these activities. Pupils learn to be painters by painting, jumpers by playing jumping games, and readers by exploring books.

Teachers are supervisors rather than instructors. They help children find things to do, maintain order, and attempt to have each child experience a variety of activities every day.

The third type of preschool is the interactive classroom, with a combined subject-centered/child-centered approach. Here children may be working in groups with some playing, some being read to by an aide, and others writing a group composition with the teacher. There are no worksheets or other drill-type material. The instruction is not the formal type of instruction like that in the bottom-up approach. It is the type of instruction you have already learned to use in nurturing your child's natural literacy.

Evaluating the approaches

Research shows that the interactive approach is the most effective for nurturing literacy because it basically teaches the appropriate skills from the "inside out." None of the preschools you observe may be pure examples of any of the models, but avoid the following if you are interested in maximizing your child's literacy:

Avoid a school in which pupils spend most of their time working in coloring books and on arithmetic and phonic worksheets. These activities are outside impositions and do not draw on a child's imagination. They create work out of what should be natural and fun.

Avoid a school in which pupils spend much of their time looking for something to do without any encouragement or organized activities provided by the teachers. You may be paying for an educational program and receiving babysitting services instead.

Here are some characteristics of schools that provide sound educational activities for children:

Instruction. Select a school in which instruction is based on skills and information that pupils acquire through their play. Teachers in these schools develop language skills by asking children to explain what they are doing, why they are doing it, and what they expect to happen during play. When instruction is based on the child's play activities, it nurtures the child's natural literacy.

School personnel. After you find a preschool program you feel comfortable with, look at the school staff. Two aspects of staffing are most important: staff qualifications and staff to child ratio. A preschool should have a full-time teacher in the classroom at all times. This teacher should hold a baccalaureate degree in education with a specialization in early childhood education or child development. Assistant teachers should have completed or be pursuing an associate degree in early childhood education or child development. Alternate qualifications, such as many years of successful work in preschools or elementary classrooms, may be acceptable substitutes for the associate degree previously mentioned.

During your visit to the school, ask about the credentials of the teacher and the staff members. Observe the personality of staff members, how they react to you, how they interact with the children, what activities are in progress in the classroom, whether children's work is displayed, whether worksheets are in use, and how well the room is equipped.

Staff to child ratio is the other aspect of staffing worth your attention. An important characteristic of a literacy-nurturing preschool is an appropriate staff to child ratio that allows individual attention. The following guidelines achieve the most effective results:

Age	Maximum group size	Staff-child ratio
Birth-2	6 children	1 staff : 3 children
2-3	12 children	1 staff : 4 children
2-5	16 children	1 staff : 8 children

It is important for preschools to have enough children for your child to learn skills such as sharing and socializing. The maximum group sizes are appropriate if the corresponding ratios are met. In that way children have the opportunity to interact, yet they are supervised closely enough so that social skills can be taught "on the spot" when called for by the situation.

Procedural activities. It is important that the classroom is pleasant, safe, and adequate for your child's needs. While visiting the school, you should notice how children and parents are greeted when they arrive. Does the teacher call everybody by name and act as if he or she is pleased to see them? Does the teacher give more attention to the children or the parents? Do the children like the teachers and assistants? Does the assistant engage a child in an activity shortly after the child arrives?

Are the toys, furniture, windows, and equipment clean? Are there cots and clean bedding for nap time? Is there a snack or are meals served? Are the menus healthful and appealing? Are diapers available for very young children? Do staff members make an effort to teach children personal grooming practices? Is discipline taught in a positive manner?

Facilities, supplies, and equipment. A good preschool must have enough space, supplies, and equipment to provide an appropriate educational program. Is the classroom large enough to accommodate three to five interest groups, a comfortable nap time, and whole-class activities such as dramatic play or storytime? Are there interest areas, such as a kitchen, library, dress-up corner, art area, sand table, building blocks, and water trough?

Is there an outside playground, and is it well equipped to encourage large muscle development? Is the equipment well maintained and safe? Is the play area fenced?

Curriculum. A preschool's curriculum determines the types of experiences and, consequently, the areas of learning for the children. Does the school program provide the equipment, materials, supplies, and opportunities necessary for children to grow in their literacy skills, fine and large motor development, creative talents, social development, and numerical concepts?

What types of learning activities are encouraged? Do the children learn through using language, creative activities, play, and social activities? Or do they fill out worksheets, color in coloring books, and, essentially, have a formal schedule that extends for most of the day? Generally speaking, a curriculum that nurtures literacy allows ample time in the school day for play activities which provide a background for learning activities that take place during the remainder of the day.

Parent accommodations. Beware of preschools that request parents not to come to the school except by appointment. Preschools should encourage a cooperative relationship among parents, staff, and children. Many preschools suggest activities parents can do at home with their children to supplement school efforts. These preschools also encourage cooperative interaction between parents and teachers and help them to work as a team in the child's education.

Discipline. Preschools should not physically punish children. With the small staff to child ratio, the teachers should be able to guide behavior without resorting to punishment.

The National Association for the Education of Young Children (NAEYC) is a professional group of early childhood educators that has set standards for the education of young children. This organization publishes information regarding preschools, the preparation of early childhood teachers, and careers in early childhood education. Two of their publications dealing with preschools are free upon request. Contact the NAEYC at 1834 Connecticut Avenue, N.W., Washington, DC. 20009-5786. The publications are *How to Choose a Good Early Childhood Program* and *Accreditation Criteria and Procedures: Position Statement of the National Academy of Early Childhood Programs.*

Postscript

*A*ll the information you need to develop your child's literacy skills is available in the chapters of this book. Use this postscript as a check list to help you remember these basic and important strategies to nurture your child's natural literacy.

■ Children's language development begins at birth.

■ You can begin helping your child's language development anytime from birth onward—the earlier the better.

■ Children who live in a language-enriched environment learn to read and write naturally.

■ Children acquire more than half their literacy skills during the first five years of their lives.

■ Because your child spends more time with you than with any other person, you are your child's first and best teacher.

- Carry on frequent conversations with your child and provide a rich selection of books to read to him or her.

- Serve as a model for your child by reading books, magazines, and newspapers regularly.

- Follow your child's lead in selecting literacy activities. By doing this you ensure that the activities are on your child's developmental level.

- Provide your child with writing tools and art materials to encourage written and visual expressions.

- Surround your child with games and building materials which encourage and develop creativity.

- Use your child's inner words to help him or her understand that written words represent spoken words and that written words communicate ideas.

- When your child learns a sufficient number of inner words, encourage him or her to form sentences with these words. Print the words and sentences in small books for your child to share with others.

- Encourage your child to write notes to friends and relatives so that they will respond with notes to him or her.

- Accept invented spelling in your child's writing. If you cannot decode it, ask the child to read it to you.

- Keep learning sessions short and let your child set the pace.

- Help develop your child's thinking skills by asking "How" and "Why" during conversations.

■ Play appropriate listening games to help your child listen carefully and follow directions.

■ Base your language activities on the knowledge that what children think about, they can talk about; what they talk about, they can write about; what they write about, they can read about.

■ Teach memory devices so that your child will have strategies for remembering important information.

■ If you enroll your child in a preschool, use the information presented in Chapter 10 to help you select a school that will nurture your child's literacy in a natural way.

■ Continue to participate in literary activities with your child even after he or she enrolls in formal schooling. You will always be your child's most important teacher!

References for Parents

Accreditation Criteria and Procedures: Position Statement of the National Academy of Early Childhood Programs (1984). National Association for the Education of Young Children. Washington, D.C.: NAEYC.

Adams, Marilyn Jager (1990). *Beginning to Read: Thinking and Learning about Print.* Massachusetts Institute of Technology Press.

Ashton-Warner, Sylvia (1963). *Teacher.* New York: Simon and Schuster.

Baghban, M. (1989). *You Can Help Your Young Child with Writing.* Newark, DE: The International Reading Association.

Bloom, Benjamin S. (1964). *Stability and Change in Human Characteristics.* New York: John Wiley & Sons, Inc.

Durkin, Delores (1966). *Children Who Read Early.* New York: Teachers College Press.

Dyson, Anne Haas (1990). *Multiple Worlds of Child Writers: Friends Learning to Write*. New York: Teachers College Press.

How to Choose a Good Early Childhood Program (1983). National Association for the Education of Young Children. Washington, D.C.: NAEYC.

Heller, Mary F. (1991). *Reading-writing Connections: From Theory to Practice*. White Plains, NY: Longman.

McGee, Lea M. and Richgels, Donald J. (1990). *Literacy's Beginnings*. Needham MA: Allyn and Bacon.

Ollila, Lloyd and Mayfield Margie I. (1992). *Emergent Literacy: Preschool, Kindergarten and Primary Grades*. Needham, MA: Allyn and Bacon.

Schweinhart, Lawrence J., and Weikart, David P. (1985). "Evidence that good early childhood programs work," *Phi Delta Kappan*, 66:545-551.

Smith, Frank (1992). "Learning to Read: The Never-Ending Debate," *Phi Delta Kappan*, 73:432-441.

Wasserman, Selma (1990). *Serious Players in the Primary Classroom: Empowering Children through Active Learning Experiences*. New York: Teachers College Press.

Books Recommended for Reading Aloud to Children

Good for children three and under

ABC by Ed Emberley: Little, Brown, 1978.

A Bedtime Story by Joan Levine: Dutton, 1975.

Abracatabby by Catherine Hiller: Coward, McCann, Geoghegan, 1981.

A Hole is to Dig by Ruth Krauss: Harper, 1952.

Ask Mr. Bear by Marjorie Flack: McMillan, 1932.

Aster Aardvark's Alphabet Adventure by Steven Kellogg: Morrow, 1987.

Bear's Adventure by Brian Wildsmith: Pantheon, 1983.

Bedtime Mouse by Sandol Stoddard: Houghton, 1982.

Boxes! Boxes! by Leonard Everett Fisher: Viking, 1984.

Brian Wildsmith's ABC by Brian Wildsmith: Franklin Watts, 1963.

City Scene from A to Z by R. Isadora: Greenwillow Books, 1984.

Do You Want to be My Friend? by Eric Carle: Thomas Y. Crowell, 1971.

Dr. Seuss's ABC by Dr. Seuss: Random House, 1963.

Early Words by Richard Scarry: Random House, 1976.

Frederick by Leo Lionni: Pantheon, 1966.

Good Dog Carl by Alexandra Day: Green Tiger Press, 1985.

Goodnight Horsey by Frank Asch: Prentice-Hall, 1981.

A Goodnight Hug by H. Roth: Grosset & Dunlap, 1986.

Goodnight Moon by Margaret Wise Brown: Harper, 1977.

Gone Fishing by Earlene Long: Houghton, 1985.

Grandma & Me by N. Ricklin, Simon and Schuster, 1988.

Guinea Pigs Far and Near by Kate Duke: E. P. Dutton, 1984.

Happy Birthday, Moon by Frank Asch: Prentice-Hall, 1982.

Henry's Busy Day by Rod Campbell: Viking Kestree, 1984.

Horse and the Bad Morning by Ted Clymer and Miska Miles: Dutton, 1983.

In the Night Kitchen by Maurice Sendak: Harper & Row, 1970.

Jump, Frog, Jump! by Robert Kalan: Greenwillow Books, 1981.

Lemon Moon by Kay Chorao: Holiday House, 1983.

Let's Make Rabbits by Leo Lionni: Pantheon Books, 1982.

Make Way for Ducklings by Robert McCloskey: Viking, 1941.

Mishka by Victor Ambius: Warne, 1978.

Moon Bear by Frank Asch: Charles Scribner's, 1978.

Moonlight by Jan Ormerod: Lothrop, 1983.

My First Picture Book by L. Weisgard, Grosset & Dunlap, 1977.

New Baby by Emily A. McCully: Harper & Row, 1988.

Of Course a Goat by Ruth Bornstein: Harper, 1980.

Oh, a'Hunting We Will Go by John Langstaff: Atheneum, 1974.

Oh, What Nonsense by William Cole: Viking, 1976.

Pat the Bunny by Dorothy Kunhardt: Golden, 1962.

Peek-A-Boo! by Janet and Allen Ahlberg: Viking, 1982.

Petunia by Roger Duvoisin: Knopf, 1950.Rabbit Finds A Way by Judy Delton: Crown, 1975.

Sniff Shout by John Murningham: Viking, 1984.

Snow by Isao Sasaki: Viking Press, 1982.

Snuffy by Dick Bruner: Methuen, 1975.

Sophie and Jack by Judy Taylor: Philomel Books, 1982.

Sun's Up by T. Euvremer: Crown, 1987.

Sunshine by Jan Ormerod: Lothrop, 1981.

The Baby Animal ABC by R. Broomfield: Penguin Books, 1976.

The Bear Who Saw the Spring by Karla Kuskin: Harper & Row, 1961.

The Blueberry Cake that Little Fox Baked by Andrea DaRif: Margaret K. McElderry Books, 1984.

The Guessing Game by Betsy and Giulio Maestro: Grosset and Dunlap, 1983.

The Little Engine that Could by Watty Piper: Platt, 1961.

The Little House by Virginia Lee Burton: Houghton Mifflin, 1942.

The Three Billy Goats Gruff by Paul Galdone: Houghton-Mifflin / Clarion Books, 1973.

The Three Little Pigs by Paul Galdone: Seabury, 1970.

The Very Hungry Caterpillar by Eric Carle: Collins, 1969.

Three Rounds with Rabbit by William H. Hooks: Lothrop, 1985.

Thump, Thump, Thump! by Anne Rockwell: E.P. Dutton, 1981.

To Bed To Bed by Misclia Richtes: Prentice-Hall, 1982.

Up and Up by Shirley Hughes: Prentice-Hall, 1929.

What's Inside? by Duanne Daughtry: Knopf, 1985.

Where's the Bear? by Charlotte Pomerantz: Greenwillow Books, 1984.

Where's Spot? by Eric Hill: Putnam, 1980.

Where the Wild Things Are by Maurice Sendak: Harper, 1963.

Wilberforce Goes on a Picnic by Margaret Gordon: Morrow, 1983.

Wynken, Blynken, and Nod by Eugene Field: Hasting's House, 1964.

Yellow Ball by Molly Bang: Morrow, 1991.

Good to read aloud to children three and older

A.B.See! by Tana Hoban: Greenwillow Books, 1983.

A Child's Garden of Verses by Robert Louis Stevenson: Franklin Watts, 1960.

A Frog Prince by Alix Berenzy: Holy, 1989.

A Giant Problem by Richard Fowler: Barron's, 1988.

Alexander and The Terrible, Horrible, No Good, Very Bad Day by Judith Viorst: Atheneum, 1976.

A Light in the Attic by Shel Silverstein: Harper, 1982.

Amos: The Story of an Old Dog and His Couch by Susan Seligson: Little Brown, 1987.

A Very Hungry Caterpillar by Eric Carle: Philomel, 1969.

Amelia Bedelia by Peggy Parrish: Scholastic, 1970.

An Egg is to Sit on by Christine Tanz: Lothrop, Lee and Shepard, 1978.

Animalia by Graeme Base: Abrams, 1987.

Are You My Mother? by Philip Eastman: Random House, 1960.

Arthur's Adventure in the Abandoned House by Fernando Krahn: E. P. Dutton, 1981.

Arthur's Halloween Costume by Lillian Hoban: Harper, 1983.

A Snake is Totally Tail by Judi Barrett: Atheneum, 1983.

A Treeful of Pigs by Arnold Lobel: Greenwillow Books, 1979.

A Walk on a Snowy Night by Judy Delton: Harper, 1983.

Babar and the Wully-Wully by Laurent De Brunhyoff: Random House, 1975.

Beast by Susan Meddaugh: Houghton Mifflin, 1981.

Bennett Cerf's Book of Animal Riddles by Bennett Cerf: Random House, 1959.

Berenstein Bear's Nursery Tales by S. and J. Berenstein: Random House, 1973.

Bertie and the Bear by Pamela Allen: Coward, 1985.

Big Al by Andrew Clements: Picture Books Studio, 1988.

Blueberries for Sal by Robert McCloskey: Viking, 1948.

Brown Bear, Brown Bear, What Do You See? by Bill Martin, Jr.: Holt Rinehart and Winston, 1983.

Cully Cully and the Bear by Wilson Gage: Greenwillow Books, 1983.

Curious George by H. A. Rey: Houghton Mifflin, 1941.

Dance Away by George Shannon: Greenwillow Books, 1982.

Deep in the Forest by Brinton Turkle: Dutton, 1976.

Dinosaur Dream by Dennis Nolan: Macmillan, 1990.

Do Not Open by Brinton Turkle: Dutton, 1982.

Don't Do That by Tony Ross: Crown, 1991.

Drawer in a Drawer by David Christiana: FS & G, 1990.

Emma's Dragon Hunt by Catherine Stock: Lothrup, 1984.

Encore for Eleanor by Bill Peet: Houghton Mifflin, 1981.

Eppie M. Says by Olivier Dunrea: MacMillan, 1990.

Ernest and Celestine by Gabrielle Vincent: Greenwillow Books, 1982.

Even If I Did Something Awful by Barbara Shook: Hazen, 1982.

Everybody Needs a Rock by Byrd Baylor: Aladdin Books, 1985.

Fireflies by Julie Brinkloe: Aladdin Books, 1989.

Fix-It by David McPhail: E. P. Dutton, 1984.

Flea Story by Robert Tallon: Holt Rinehart and Winston, 1977.

Flossie and the Fox by Patricia McKissack: Knopf, 1988.

Foolish Rabbit's Big Mistake by Rafe Martin: Putnam, 1985.

Gaston the Green-Nosed Alligator by James Rice: Pelecin, 1982.

Grandpa's Face by Eloise Greenfield.

Hailstones and Halibut Bones by Mary O'Neill: Doubleday, 1961.

Hairy Maclary from Donaldson's Dairy by Lynley Dodd: Gareth Stevens, 1985.

Hairy Maclary's Rumpus at the Vet by Lynley Dodd: Gareth Stevens,1990.

Hairy Maclary, Scattercat by Lynley Dodd: Gareth Stevens, 1988.

Hans Andersen–His Classic Fairy Tales translated by Erik Hagwood: Doubleday, 1976.

Harold's Runaway Nose by Harriet Sonnenschein: Simon and Schuster,1989.

Harry the Dirty Dog by Gene Zion: Harper, 1956.

Hattie and the Fox by Mem Fox: Bradbury, 1986.

Hazel's Amazing Mother by Rosemary Wells: Dial, 1985.

Henry and the Dragon by Eileen Christelow: Clarion, 1984.

Hey, Al by Arthur Yorinks: F, S & G, 1991.

Hi, Cat by Ezra Jack Keats: Macmillan, 1970.

Hildegard Sings by Thomas Wharton: F, S & G, 1991.

Household Stories of the Brothers Grimm translated by Lucy Crane: Dover, 1963.

If I Ran the Zoo by Dr. Seuss: Random House, 1950.

I Know A Lady by James Stevenson: Greenwillow Books, 1985.

I'll Fix Anthony by Judith Viorst: Harper, 1969.

In a Dark, Dark Room and Other Scary Stories by Alvin Schwartz: Harper & Row, 1984.

Impossible Possum by Ellen Concord: Little, Brown, 1971.

I Wouldn't Be Scared by John Sabraw: Orchard, 1989.

Jonah and the Great Fish by Warwick Hutton: Margaret K. McEldessy Books, 1983.

Joyful Noise: Poems for Two Voices by Paul Fleischman: Harper & Row, 1988.

Just a Dream by Chris Allsbury: Houghton Mifflin, 1990.

King Henry's Palace by Pat Hutchins: Greenwillow Books, 1983.

Knots on a Country Rope by Bill Martin Jr.: Henry Holt, 1987.

Laura's Story by Beatrice S. DeRegniers: Atheneum, 1979.

Lentil by Robert McCloskey: Viking, 1940.

Lester's Overnight by Kay Chorao: Dutton, 1977.

Listen to the Rain by Bill Martin Jr. and John Archambault: Henry Holt, 1988.

Little Bear by Else Holmelund Minarik: Harper & Row, 1957.

Little Mouse, the Red Ripe Strawberry and the Big Hungry Bear by Don and Audrey Wood: Child's Play, 1984.

Little Tim and the Brave Sea Captain by Edward Ardizzone: Oxford 1936.

Little Toot by Hardie Gramatky: Putnam, 1939.

Lon Po Po by Ed Young: Philomel, 1989.

Lost in the Museum by Miriam Cohen: Greenwillow Books, 1978.

Madeline by Ludwig Bendmans: Simon & Schuster, 1939.

Mama Don't Allow by Thatcher Hurd: Harper & Row, 1984.

Mary Had a Little Lamb by Sara Josepha Hale: Holiday House, 1984.

Max by Giovannetti: Atheneum, 1977.

Meanwhile Back at the Ranch by Trinka Hakes Noble: Dial, 1987.

Messy Baby by Jan Ormerod: Lathrop, Lee & Shepard, 1984.

Midnight Farm by Reeve Lindbergh: Dial, 1987.

Mike Mulligan and His Steam Shovel by Virginia Lee Burton: Houghton Mifflin, 1939.

Millions of Cats by Wanda Gag: Coward-McGann, 1928.

Mr. Little's Noisy Car by Richard Fowler: Grosset & Dunlap, 1985.

My Grandfather's Journey by John Cech: Bradbury, 1991.

Napping House by Audrey Wood: HBJ, 1984.

Nettie Jo's Friends by Patricia McKissack: Knopf, 1989.

Noah's Ark by Peter Spier: Doubleday, 1977.

Nobody Listens to Andrew by Elizabeth Guilfoile: Follett, 1957.

No Elephants Allowed by Deborah Robison: Houghton Mifflin, 1982.

Norman the Doorman by Don Freeman: Viking, 1959.

Now We Are Six by A. A. Milne: Dutton, 1927.

Ol'Jake's Lucky Day by Anatoly Ivanov: Lothrop, 1984.

One Hunter by Pat Hutchins: Greenwillow Books, 1982.

On Market Street by Arnold Lobel: Greenwillow Books, 1982.

One Kitten for Kim by Adelaide Hall, Addison-Wesley, 1969.

Our King Has Horns by Richard Pevear: MacMillan, 1987.

Oval Moon by Jane Yolen: Philomel, 1987.

Peter and the Wolf by Sergei Prokofiev: Viking, 1982.

Piper, Pipe that Song Again collected by Nancy Larrick: Random House, 1965.

Poem Stew by William Cole: Lippincott, 1982.

Pulling My Leg by Jo Carson: Orchard, 1990.

Ragtime Trumpie by Alan Schroeder: Little Brown, 1989.

Regards to the Man in the Moon by Ezra Jack Keats: Four Winds, 1981.

Saint George and the Dragon by Margaret Hodges: Little, Brown,1984.

Sarah's Unicorn by Bruce and Katherine Coville: Lippincott, 1979.

See My Lovely Poison Ivy by Lilian Moore: Atheneum, 1975.

Seven in One Blow by Freire Wright and Michael Foreman: Random, 1982.

Stone Soup by Marcia Brown: Charles Scribner's Sons, 1947.

Strega Nona by Tomie De Paola: Prentice-Hall, 1975.

Sylvester and the Magic Pebble by William Steig: Simon & Schuster, 1969.

Take Another Look by Tana Hoban: Greenwillow Books, 1982.

Tallyho, Pinkerton! by Steven Kellogg: Dial, 1983.

That Terrible Halloween Night by James Stevenson: Greenwillow Books, 1980.

The Adventures of Paddy Pork by John S. Goodall: Harcourt, 1968.

The Aesop for Children, pictures by Milo Winter: Rand McNally & Co., 1919.

The Banza by Diane Wolkstein: Dial, 1982.

The Boy Who Was Followed Home by Margaret Maby: Dial Press, 1975.

The Carrot Seed by Ruth Krauss: Harper & Row, 1945.

The Caterpillar and the Polliwog by Jack Kent: Prentice, 1983.

The Comic Adventures of Old Mother Hubbard and Her Dog by Tomie De Paola: Harcourt, 1981.

The Contests at Cowlick by Richard Kennedy: Little, Brown, 1975.

The Day the Teacher Went Bananas by James Howe: E. P. Dutton, 1984.

The Doorbell Rang by David Christiana: F, S & G, 1990.

The Frog Prince Continued by Jon Scieszka: Viking, 1991.

The Giant's Toe by Brock Cole: F, S & G, 1986.

The Giving Tree by Shel Silverstein: Harper, 1964.

The Golden Treasury of Poetry edited by Louis Unter-meyer: Golden, 1959.

The House on East 88th Street by Bernard Waber: Houghton Mifflin, 1962.

The Hungry Thing Returns by Jan Slepian and Ann Seidler: Scholastic, 1990.

The Hunter and the Animals by Tomie de Paola: Holiday House, 1981.

The Incredible Painting of Felix Clousseau by Jon Agee: F, S & G,1988.

The Island of the Skog by Steven Kellogg: Dial, 1973.

The Man Who Kept House by Kathleen and Michael Hague: Harcourt, 1982.

The Marvelous Catch of Old Hannibal by Berthe Amoss: Parent's Magazine Press, 1970.

The Mother Goose Treasury by Ramond Briggs: Coward-McCann, 1966.

The Mysterious Tadpole by Steven Kellogg: Dial, 1977.

The Night After Christmas by James Stevenson: Greenwillow Books, 1982.

The Quilt by Ann Jonas: Greenwillow Books, 1984.

The Reason for the Pelican by John Ciardi: Lippincott, 1969.

There's a Party at Mona's Tonight by Harry Allard: Doubleday, 1981.

The Secret Birthday Message by Eric Carle: Crowell, 1972.

The Silver Pony by Lynd Ward: Houghton Mifflin, 1973.

The Story of Ferdinand by Munro Leaf: Viking, 1936.

The Tale of Peter Rabbit and Other Stories by Beatrix Potter: Alfred A. Knopf, 1984.

The Teeny-Tiny Woman: A Ghost Story by Paul Galdone: Clarion Books, 1984.

The Turtle and the Monkey by Paul Galdone: Clarion Books, 1983.

The Velveteen Rabbit by Margey Williams: Alfred A. Knoff, 1986.

The Very Quiet Cricket by Eric Carle: Philomel, 1990.

The Winter Wren by Brock Cole: Farrar, Straus & Giroux, 1984.

The Witches by Roald Dahl: Farrar, Straus & Giroux, 1983.

The World of Christopher Robin by A. A. Milne: E.P. Dutton, 1958.

True Story of the 3 Little Pigs by Tomie De Paola: Viking Kestrel,1989.

26 Letters and 99 Cents by Tana Hoban: Greenwillow Books, 1987.

Tyrannosaurus Was a Beast by Jack Prelutsky: Morrow, 1988.

We Can't Sleep by James Stevenson: Greenwillow Books, 1983.

We Were Tired of Living in a House by Liesce Moak Skorpen: Coward-McCann, 1969.

Whatever Happened to Dinosaurs? by Bernard Most: Harcourt, 1985.

What Happens Next? by Jania Domanska: Greenwillow Books, 1983.

What's in Fox's Sack? by Paul Galdone: Clarion, 1983.

When I Was Young in the Mountains by Cynthia Rylant: E. F. Dutton, 1982.

Where the River Begins by Thomas Locker: Dial, 1984.

Where the Sidewalk Ends by Shel Silverstein: Harper & Row, 1974.

Who Sank the Boat? by Pamela Allen: Coward-McCann, 1983.

William's Doll by Charlotte Zoltow: Harper Row, 1972.

You Make the Angels Cry by Denys Cazet: Bradbury Press, 1983.

Yuck! by James Stevenson: Greenwillow Books, 1984.